A Taste of Africa

A Taste of Africa

of Africa

Traditional & Modern African Cooking

DORINDA HAFNER

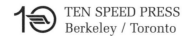

TEN SPEED PRESS
Berkeley / Toronto

*To my goddaughter and niece, Nikita Naa Abia Catherine Shaw
and my daddy — you will live in my heart forever.*

A Kirsty Melville Book

Ten Speed Press
P.O. Box 7123
Berkeley, California 94707
www.tenspeed.com

Distributed in Canada by Ten Speed Press Canada, in South Africa by Real Books, in Southeast Asia by Berkeley Books, and in the United Kingdom and Europe by Airlift Book Company.

Design by Betsy Stromberg
Food photography, front and back cover, by Jonathan Chester/Extreme Images
Author photograph by Adam Haddrick
Front cover: Moors and Christians (page 204); back cover: Okra Stew (page 12)

Library of Congress Cataloging-in-Publication Data

Hafner, Dorinda.
A taste of Africa: traditional and modern African cooking/ Dorinda Hafner
p.cm.
Includes bibliographic references and index.
ISBN 1-58008-403-6
1. Cookery, African. 2. Africa-Social life and customs. I. Title.
TX725.A4 H35 2002
641.596-dc21
2002023326

First printing, 2002
Printed in Singapore

1 2 3 4 5 6 7 8 9 10 — 06 05 04 03 02

Contents

Acknowledgments

To the following people I give my most heartfelt thanks:

Alex Moshe (Tanzania) I can now boast of more than two words of Swahili.

Annette Holton (Trinidad and Tobago) Your recipes are as hybrid and rich as yourself.

Augustine Mpofu (Zimbabwe) Your sense of humor and ubiquitous behavior kept "Queen Bulabula" amused through difficult times.

Beatrice Howarth (Egypt) For your warmth, support and wicked sense of humor, my soul sister!

Mrs. Elizabeth Addy (Ghana) My mother—the person who started it all, and who gave me the knowledge and love of diverse foods. Mom, I love you.

Eileen Haley (Spanish consultant) The lynchpin between Mrs. Marchanté and me. I promise to learn Spanish!

Mrs. Emilia Marchanté (Cuba) Dear Emilia, we deserve medals for wonderful cross-cultural communication: my negligible Spanish and your sparse English.

Felipe Lincy (Guadeloupe) The elusive, comical French friend who kept my interest in Guadeloupe alive.

James and Nuala Hafner My beautiful children—for your eternal patience and willingness to taste almost everything I cooked! Thank you for believing in me and for your love and support.

Dr. Kwame Asumadu (Ghana) My expert on Ashanti culture—for your generosity and warmth.

Lucia V. Rodrigues (Brazil) For your speed in introducing me to Brazilian recipes, which have traveled halfway across the world.

Mike and Jenny Piper (Kenya) Kenya will always be alive wherever you two go: "sukuma Wiki."

Jigzie Campbell (Jamaica) This is "Fe we Africa/ Jamaica connection—how we tek bad ting mek joke!"

Mrs. Rita Pike and Ms. Marlene Black (Jamaica) Your wholesome Jamaican recipes have become family treasures.

Natasha Koodravsev-Boyar (Australia) Thank you for your continued support, advice, encouragement, and above all, friendship.

Sofia Poppe (Tanzania) The Tanzanian beauty with a magic touch in the kitchen. Thank you for your wonderful recipes.

Kirsty Melville (America) My determined publisher (who also published the first edition of this book). Thank you for your faith and for never taking "no" for an answer.

Windy Ferges (America) The mistress of clever cajoling. Thank you for your encouragement, patience, and discipline while editing my book.

Betsy Stromberg (America) Thank you for including a large part of my heritage in your beautiful design for my book.

To all my friends—too numerous to mention—whose combined presence and nurturing have been invaluable.

Foreword

There is a famous saying that "Africa always offers something new."

Nowhere is this better expressed than in Dorinda Hafner's wonderful book, *A Taste of Africa.* In her selection of recipes and her recollections of the way of life and the foods of the countries she loves, Dorinda creates a portrait of Africa that is vital and interesting.

Whether she is telling a legend from a particular country, tracing the African influence on the food and culture of the Caribbean and the Americas, or describing with great enthusiasm the delights of particular ingredients and recipes that are unusual to many Western cooks, Dorinda captures the smells, the sounds, and the tastes of Africa.

I recently made my first journey to South Africa—a very exciting, stimulating, and moving experience. You don't have to go that far to be captivated by *A Taste of Africa.*

—WHOOPI GOLDBERG

Introduction

Although I am an African born and bred in Africa, I have lived on four continents and visited many countries around the world. Over the years I have seen and heard many Africans actively or passively denounce their roots in preference for different cultures. While intercultural exchanges are healthy and should be encouraged, I remain immensely proud of my origins. For me, Africa continues to be as enigmatic and fascinating from within as from without.

A Taste of Africa is my modest contribution to the continent of my birth and to the stoic, quiet achievers who daily instill in the children of Africa the values of Africa's inherent wealth and a respect for a continent long designated as "primitive," but which continues to shock and excite. What better way is there than with the double-edged sword of Africa's food—the variety, the diversity, and quality of it in parts, and the lack of it in others.

Africa is making news worldwide, warts and all, with its colorful cultural splendors, its hunger, drought, and politics. Africa is indeed enigmatic. The continent can boast some of the most exciting cuisine in the world and yet, paradoxically and tragically, some parts of it are starving. Perhaps by showing the world the positive picture of African cuisine I might in some small way highlight the plight of the starving millions on our continent and approach the problem from a different angle. "The way to people's hearts is through their stomachs" is, in this context, a weird paradox indeed!

Parts of Africa, due to natural disasters, the fickleness of the elements, internecine conflicts, and other circumstances, are experiencing phenomenal shortages of food crops, agricultural materials, water, and other necessities fundamental to sustaining life. But this does not mean that when and where these "raw materials" are available Africa cannot boast of "cuisines par excellence," easily standing alongside Asia, Europe, and others of the world's best exponents of good food. The time has come to elucidate and elevate African cuisine to international status and to reintroduce both Africans and non-Africans alike to the intrinsic values of good, wholesome, and tasty eating—the African way!

A Taste of Africa looks at food from ten different African countries, each of which is representative of food from its specific region of Africa, and from those countries across the Atlantic where African food has made itself at home since the iniquitous slave-trading era. Among the African countries themselves, this book highlights both the similarity and diversity of preparation and cooking styles, such as the mixture of sweet and savory in a main meal by the inclusion of fresh and dried fruits in North African cuisine, as opposed to the combination of meat, fish, and vegetables in a single soup or stew as practiced in countries south of the Sahara. Add to these continental differences the exciting changes that have transformed original African recipes into hybrid, culinary masterpieces by the integration of Portuguese, Spanish, French, Dutch,

Arawak, and Carib Indian cooking traditions in places like South and Central America, the West Indies, and Lousiana, and you begin to understand why I have chosen to write such a book. Investigating the similarities as well as the differences has been fascinating and exciting. I hope that this book will be both an invaluable addition to any personal cookbook collection and a useful guide to African food for academic and teaching institutions.

I had enormous difficulty in choosing the recipes because I wanted to pick those that, while easy to follow, made distinct statements about their African origins and at the same time showed the new cultural influences. Superficially this should have been easy, but some of my favorite recipes, once typed, sounded and looked unpalatable, and my "guinea pig" friends refused to try them!

Then there was the question of whether or not to include some of the more boring, although traditionally staple, African recipes, as well as the problem of major regional variations within the African continent itself. For example, because of the physical nature of the regions, more fish is consumed in West Africa than meat, and more meat is consumed in East Africa than fish.

I also had to consider the problem of repetition since most of the ingredients are common to all the black cultures in question. Produce such as corn, cassava, plantains, beans, and okra are staple components of most African cuisines and appear in recipes that may seem quite similar, yet also display regional and cultural variation. The continued inclusion of palm oil (*dende* oil) in Latin, Central, and North American cuisines as well as in the Caribbean, plus the similarity of methods of food preparation in dishes like *fufu* (*foo-foo* in Trinidad and Tobago); *funchu* in Curaçao; *dokono* in Jamaica; *caruru, vatapa,* and *serapatel* in Brazil; *moros y cristianos con platanos* in Cuba; and dirty rice and gumbo in Louisiana, confirms the obvious cultural connections. They also mark the distinct differences between Western dishes and cooking styles and the African style of cooking.

Other differences between Western and African treatments of food are obvious. In parts of Africa, quite heavy, savory meals are eaten for breakfast before departing for work in the mornings—foods such as Tom Brown or black-eyed beans with rice or *gari*—a practice generally foreign to Westerners. Another major difference in eating habits is that meat is usually treated as a flavoring in African cooking and does not necessarily constitute the bulk of the main meal. I have only included a few recipes for sweets or desserts in this book to establish that they do exist as part of African cuisine. For traditional cultural reasons, Africans south of the Sahara do not usually encourage desserts and sweets.

I have had enormous problems trying to translate my typically African "let's estimate" style of cooking into easy-to-follow, easy-to-identify Western recipes. My mother and her mother before her have always cooked straight from their hearts, and this is the way I cook, too. I assumed it was going to be really easy to write for an audience to follow suit. What a rude awakening! In order to introduce traditional African cooking into modern kitchens, I have had to learn how to measure ingredients and give specific cooking temperatures and times—that is the hardest thing of all for me. Many are the times at the butcher's that I have felt tempted to grab two chickens, one in each hand, to ascertain their comparative weights—the traditional way to determine how many people each bird would feed.

While I make no apologies for what I have written, I must be honest and tell you that I have tried as hard as I am able to give explanations for my modus operandi and to measure most things for you, but I invite you to try to maintain the emotion and flow of African cooking. If you have never cooked intuitively before, here's your chance. Use common sense, your eyes, and the feel of things to arrive at the correct amounts you need; if you normally cook like this, then roll up your sleeves and go for it.

I hope you will have as much fun cooking and eating African food as I have had preparing it for, presenting it to, and sharing it with you.

GHANA

OFFICIAL TITLE: Republic of Ghana

CAPITAL CITY: Accra

OFFICIAL LANGUAGE: English, although Akan, Ewe, Ga, and Massi-Dagomba are widely spoken

CURRENCY: Ghanaian Cedi (C) = 100 pesewas

CASH CROPS FOR EXPORT: Cocoa, coffee, palm oil, copra, cola nuts, shea butter. kenaf (the fiber is used like jute), and limes

FOOD CROPS: Cassava, corn, millet, sorghum, rice, plantains, yams, poultry, and fish

TOTAL LAND AREA: 92,665 square miles

Peanut Soup with Guinea Fowl and Dumplings

Though the poultry traditionally used in this dish is guinea fowl, the meat of which is dark, you may substitute chicken. Processed poultry will disintegrate quickly in the soup, so once it is cooked, remove it from the pot until the soup has thickened. But do leave it long enough for the peanut and vegetable mixture to permeate the meat. Peanuts, known as groundnuts in Africa, provide the rich flavor and creamy texture of this soup.

This soup is usually served with fufu, *an Akan dumpling made from yams, taro root, plantains, cassava, or even processed potato flakes. The* fufu *should sit like an island in a sea of soup, with the meat and fish scattered over the top. It is even referred to as the "island in the sun"! This dish is traditionally eaten with your fingers—even the soup!*

SERVES 4

6 to 8 guinea fowl or chicken pieces, or 2 pounds (1 kg) lean meat (such as chops or medallions of lamb shanks), cut into chunks

Salt

Freshly ground black pepper

2 large yellow onions, minced

4 large, very ripe tomatoes, or 2 cups canned whole tomatoes, drained and puréed

1 cup peanut paste or peanut butter

8 cups boiling water

Red chiles, fresh or dried, ground, for seasoning (optional)

4 to 8 mushrooms, cleaned (optional)

2 pounds (1 kg) fish fillets, salted, smoked, grilled, deep-fried, or sundried

Potato Dumplings (page 20)

Put the poultry or meat in a very large, heavy-based pan (not a crockpot, because the initial cooking process requires fairly high heat, which a crockpot does not provide). Season the meat with salt and pepper. Add the onions, stir, and cook "dry" on medium heat, stirring continuously, until the outside of the meat is slightly cooked and browned on all sides.

Pour the tomato purée into the meat and onion mixture, and continue to simmer.

Put the peanut paste in a big bowl, add 2¼ cups of the boiling water, and use a wooden spoon or a blender to blend the paste and water carefully together to form a creamy, smooth sauce.

Add the peanut sauce to the meat mixture, as well as the chiles and mushrooms. Continue to simmer, stirring only occasionally to prevent the food from sticking to the bottom of the pan. This is the basic soup. Pour the rest of the boiling water into the soup, and simmer slowly on medium heat to cook the meat for 30 to 40 minutes, depending on the type of meat used (guinea fowl takes about 10 minutes longer).

Prepare your choice of fish by removing any residual bones. Add the fish, either whole or in chunks, to the soup during the last 30 minutes of cooking time to prevent it from breaking up in the soup. Once you add all the ingredients, simmer slowly until the soup thickens. Serve with the dumplings.

Ham Soup with Basil and Vegetables

This is an easy, affordable, and deliciously tasty soup. In fact, it is one of my family's favorite foods. Indeed, some members of my family would eat this soup with my fufu (dumplings) three times daily if they could, and that includes me! This soup cooks best in a pressure cooker; if you have one, use it for this recipe.

SERVES 4 TO 6

6 dried shiitake mushrooms

2 pounds (4 kg) smoked, meaty ham shank (choose the meaty, flat, rib portions, cut into 3-inch squares by your butcher)

6 large tomatoes, blanched and peeled, or 1 13-ounce (410-g) can Italian peeled tomatoes

3 large yellow or red onions, coarsely diced

2 tablespoons tomato paste

12 cups water (10 cups if using pressure cooker)

3 large sprigs basil

2 potatoes, peeled and quartered

1 large zucchini, coarsely diced

1 large carrot, peeled and cut into 6 pieces

2 or 3 hot chiles (such as habanero, Scotch bonnet, or Thai) (optional)

Place the dried shiitake mushrooms in a small bowl of water and soak them overnight. Drain before using.

Trim any excess fat, sinew, or bone debris from the ham shank. Wash and place them in a large pressure cooker or stockpot (4- to 5-quart capacity).

In small batches, blend together the tomatoes, onions, and tomato paste with 4 cups of the water. Pour the mixture over the ham.

If using a pressure cooker, add the basil, potatoes, zucchini, carrot, mushrooms, chiles, and the remaining water. Close the lid and cook according to the appliance instructions. However, this soup must be cooked at least 1 hour. After cooking, pressure cookers take a long time to cool down before they can be opened.

If using a stockpot, add the remaining water and 2 sprigs of basil. Bring to a rolling boil on high heat, then decrease the heat to medium-low. Boil gently for about 40 minutes, or until the meat between the ham shank starts to soften. Add the third sprig of basil, the potatoes, zucchini, carrot, mushrooms, and chiles. Continue boiling until all the ingredients are well done and the meat on the ham shank is cooked and very tender. The soup should be runny but creamy and thick with vegetable pieces for texture. If it is too thick, however, the saltiness of the ham shank will take over. Add more water as necessary.

Once the soup is ready, use a slotted spoon to carefully remove the hot chiles. Serve hot, but do not remove the bones; allow your guests to enjoy the meat on the bones by using their fingers when the soup cools.

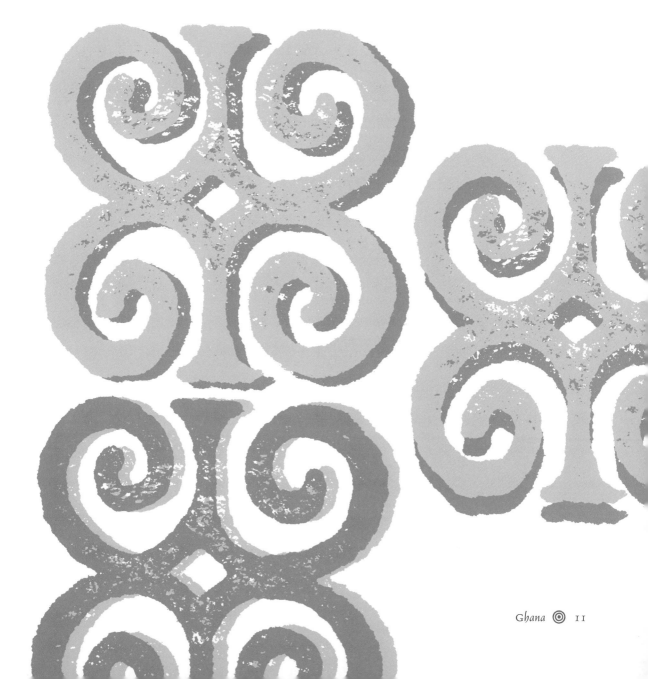

Okra Stew

Only every so often in my life have I come across a dish that seems to surfeit all my senses! This stew is one. With its clever mix of seafood, smoked ham, dried salted fish, and vegetables such as okra, eggplant, tomatoes, and onions, it smells good, tastes sensational, and even feels good, with a wonderful smooth texture. I always feel that this food can win wars! This stew is delicious with a variety of carbohydrates, such as boiled rice, Cornmeal Dumplings (page 21), boiled potatoes, yams, taro root, plantains, cassava, or gari (page 221).

SERVES 4

1 pound (500 g) okra

1¼ cups oil, preferably palm oil (see Note)

3 or 4 yellow onions, minced

2 eggplants, peeled and finely diced

Pinch of ground *kaawé* or traditional stone, thought to enhance the "tackiness" of the okra (optional)

4 tablespoons peeled and grated fresh ginger

1 to 4 fresh red chiles, minced (optional)

4 large, ripe tomatoes, blanched, peeled, and puréed, or 1 cup canned tomatoes, mashed

½ cup dried shrimp

1 ounce (30 g) dried salted fish (such as herring), shredded

Small piece of cured, salted beef (optional)

¼ pound (125 g) smoked ham, diced, and/or 4 small pieces of boiled pig's feet (substitute another meat, more fish, or crab, but not chicken)

Trim the ends of the okra, and slice the pods into thin rounds. In a large, heavy pan, heat the oil and fry the onions until they are light brown. Stirring constantly, add the okra, eggplant, *kaawé*, ginger, chiles, and tomatoes, allowing 3 minutes simmering time between each addition. This dish burns easily, so stir regularly.

Simmer about 10 minutes on low heat. Add the dried shrimp, dried salted fish, salted beef, smoked ham, and pig's feet. Simmer 10 to 15 minutes, or until all the ingredients are well blended and cooked, but not mushy.

This dish should be served hot.

NOTE: If you use plain vegetable oil, add 4 teaspoons ground turmeric.

Toasted Cornmeal Porridge

TOM BROWN

Many West African schoolchildren call this dish Tom Brown, while others call it Laying Concrete. The former name was coined from the book, Tom Brown's School Days, *because the recipe is so often served at boarding school.*

When made properly (as opposed to the lumpish mass I remember being dished up at school), it is absolutely delicious and quite addictive. For this dish, it's always better to use freshly roasted and ground corn, if only for the smell alone!

SERVES 4

2 cups *ablémamu* (finely ground, roasted corn)

3¹/₂ cups milk, hot

8 teaspoons brown sugar , or more, according to taste

To make the *ablémamu*, dry-roast 2¹/₂ cups ordinary popcorn kernels. Remove from the heat just before the popcorn begins to pop, then cool and grind until powdery and fine in a spice or coffee grinder. Cool overnight.

Place the *ablémamu* in 4 cereal bowls. In each bowl, pour in a portion of the hot milk and add some of the sugar. Stir to mix thoroughly. It will thicken and swell to form a typical Tom Brown porridge. Sit back, smell it, tuck in, and . . . enjoy.

The Legend of the Golden Stool

The Ashanti of Ghana are part of a larger group of Akan-speaking peoples. Centuries ago, wars periodically broke out between the different kingdoms of these people, and the custom was for the loser to send a member of his royal household to serve the victor in his kingdom.

The kingdom of Denkyira annexed the budding Ashanti kingdom, and the Ashanti prince Osei-Tutu was sent to wait on the Denkyiran king Nana Boa Amponsem. In Denkyira, a fetish priest named Okomfo Anokye, who had come from the kingdom of Akwamu, befriended Osei-Tutu.

As the Ashanti was, and still is, a matriarchal society, when the king of the Ashanti died, his maternal nephew Osei-Tutu was called home to assume the throne. He asked to take Okomfo Anokye with him. In time Okomfo Anokye became the most influential high priest of the Ashanti, giving spiritual protection to the kingdom.

To cement his friendship with King Osei-Tutu, Okomfo Anokye decided to conjure from the heavens a solid gold stool with the power to make the Ashanti invincible.

As part of the eight-day ritual, he took two saplings of a native *kum* tree and planted them some distance apart, proclaiming that whichever lived would mark the site of the new capital of the kingdom.

Okomfo Anokye then took the *akonfena*, the sword of state, and marked a spot where a hole was to be dug in which he would be buried. While entombed he would consult the tribal elders who had preceded him and would receive supernatural powers to pass on to the Ashanti.

He charged everyone not to cry if he did not return in eight days, for, he explained, he could only return if no tears were shed. Before his burial he promised that on the third day, the golden stool would descend from heaven.

Legend has it that this is exactly what happened, but tragically, when Okomfo Anokye had not reappeared by the eighth day, the Ashanti women began to wail, and he was lost forever.

The sapling that lived marked the capital of the new kingdom, which was called Kumasi (which means "under *kum*") and is still the capital of the Ashanti today. The place where the other sapling died marks the present-day town of Kumawu. To this day the sword of state remains inextricable from the ground into which Okomfo Anokye thrust it, and many believe the golden stool, the symbol of the Ashanti power, rests at the Ashanti palace.

Palava Sauce

There are many variations of this traditional spinach dish from West Africa. No one can agree about its origins—some say it is Nigerian, others claim it comes from Ghana, but my mother says her version comes from Sierra Leone!

In West Africa palava *means "business or trouble," so I suppose you can also call this dish Trouble Sauce. Actually, it is a stew rather than a sauce, a rich blend of spinach, pumpkin seeds, shrimp, meat, and fish. Despite its name, it is no trouble to cook and certainly no trouble to eat!*

This dish is delicious served with boiled rice, yams, plantains, gari *(page 221), Cornmeal Dumplings (page 21), or any root vegetable, roasted, boiled or grilled.*

SERVES 4

1 cup palm oil (see Note)

4 yellow onions, minced

4 large tomatoes, blanched, peeled, and mashed

2 to 4 fresh red chiles, minced (optional)

Salt

Freshly ground black pepper

1/2 pound (250 g) diced cooked meat (not chicken), and/or 1/2 pound (250 g) fish (such as snapper or pompano)

1/4 pound (125 g) smoked herring, boneless (optional)

3/4 cup dried shrimp

3 bunches fresh spinach, chopped, or 1 1/2 pounds (750 g) frozen chopped spinach

1/2 cup pumpkin seeds, ground in a spice or coffee grinder

Heat the oil in a medium pan and fry the onions until golden. Add the tomatoes and the chiles, and season with pepper. Cook for 10 to 15 minutes on low heat, stirring regularly (not continuously).

Season with salt and add the diced meat and/or fish. Stir in the smoked herring and the dried shrimp. Simmer on very low heat, stirring regularly to prevent burning.

Add the spinach to the meat mixture. Cover and simmer on low heat for 10 to 15 minutes, or until the spinach is soft and cooked. Stir regularly, taking care not to break up the fish too much.

Add the pumpkin seeds and stir them into the sauce. Cook for another 10 to 15 minutes on low heat, or until the sauce is thick and green. It will be speckled white with the ground pumpkin seeds.

NOTE: Palm oil is red oil from the red, tropical palm kernel. It is used for making a variety of foods, including some graham crackers. Substitute corn or vegetable oil and 4 teaspoons ground turmeric to give a similar look and taste.

Chile Sambal

Many African recipes combine filling, although rather bland, dishes made from grains or vegetables with spicy sauces, soups, and condiments to provide the flavor. Chile sambal is one of these zesty additions, and you can use it to pep up not only grain- or vegetable-based dishes, but also seafood, poultry, and meat recipes. Here are three sambal recipes known collectively as "shitor." Fresh Chile Sambal will keep for only a day or two; Traditional Dark Chile Sambal and Dorinda's Chile Sambal will keep in the refrigerator for up to a year.

MAKES ABOUT 6 CUPS

**TRADITIONAL DARK
CHILE SAMBAL**

1 1/2 cups vegetable oil

4 yellow onions, minced

1/2 cup peeled and finely
    grated fresh ginger

2 tablespoons tomato paste

2 chicken bouillon cubes

3/4 cup dried shrimp

1/2 cup tiny dried shrimp,
    ground to a powder

1/3 cup chile powder

Heat the oil in a heavy-based medium pan and fry the onions and ginger for 10 to 15 minutes, or until the onions are golden. Stir in the tomato paste and mix thoroughly.

Crush the chicken bouillon cubes, add them to the pan, and stir to mix. Simmer, stirring frequently, for 3 minutes. Add both types of shrimp and stir for 1 minute. Add the chile powder and thoroughly blend. Cook for 2 more minutes, stirring continuously. Be careful not to burn the mixture at this stage.

Remove from the heat and let stand for about 1 hour, or until cool. Transfer to a storage jar, and keep in a cool place.

MAKES ABOUT 2 1/2 CUPS

FRESH CHILE SAMBAL

6 fresh red chiles, minced

1 yellow onion, minced

3 large tomatoes, blanched,
    peeled, and chopped

Salt

Combine the chiles, onion, and tomatoes in a bowl, and mash or process to a pulp. Season with salt and serve as a side dish or sauce.

MAKES ABOUT 6 CUPS

DORINDA'S CHILE SAMBAL

1$\frac{1}{2}$ cups vegetable oil

8 cloves garlic, minced

4 yellow onions, minced

$\frac{1}{2}$ cup coarsely grated fresh
  ginger (peeled or unpeeled)

2 tablespoons tomato paste

2 chicken bouillon cubes

$\frac{3}{4}$ cup dried shrimp

$\frac{1}{2}$ cup dried tiny shrimp

$\frac{1}{2}$ cup chile powder

Heat the oil in a heavy-based medium pan and fry the garlic, onions, and ginger for 10 to 15 minutes, until the onions are golden. Stir in the tomato paste and mix thoroughly.

Crush the chicken bouillon cubes, add them to the pan, and stir to mix. Add both amounts of dried shrimp and stir for 1 minute. Add the chile powder and mix thoroughly.

Remove from the heat and let stand for about 1 hour, or until cool. Transfer to a storage jar, and keep in a cool place.

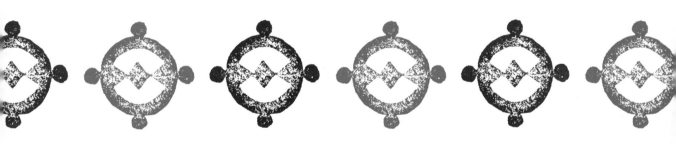

Ghanaian Salad

The kaleidoscope of colors brought to this dish by the wonderful variety of ingredients only hints at its exciting combination of textures and flavors. With eggs, fish, and a wide range of fresh vegetables, the salad is delicious and healthy and a meal on its own served with warm herb bread and chilled water garnished with watercress or basil.

SERVES 8

2 large red onions, sliced into very thin rings

Red wine or cider vinegar, for marinating

1 cucumber

1 head romaine lettuce

2 cups canned baked beans

2 cups canned salmon or other oily fish, drained

2 cups canned corn kernels, drained

1 cup mayonnaise

1/2 cup soy milk

1/4 pound (125 g) snow peas, topped and tailed

4 firm, ripe tomatoes, sliced into rounds

1 avocado, sliced (optional)

4 potatoes or yams, peeled, boiled, and diced

3 hard-boiled eggs, sliced into rounds

Marinate the onions in vinegar for 30 minutes. With a fork, deeply score the cucumber vertically, along the sides from top to bottom, then slice it thinly into rounds. Cut the lettuce in half vertically and then into thin half-moon strips.

Place the baked beans in one bowl and the salmon in another bowl. Put the corn in a third bowl. Blend the mayonnaise with the soy milk to use as dressing.

Using a huge, preferably deep and oval-shaped salad dish, arrange alternate layers of all the ingredients and dressing until you use most of the ingredients. Leave some egg, snow peas, and dressing to finish it aesthetically. Store in the refrigerator for at least 1 hour before serving. You can also make the salad the day before it is to be served, if it is refrigerated. When ready to serve, slice it like a cake, lift out portions, and serve with your favorite bread.

Fried Plantains

Everybody knows about bananas, yet surprisingly I still come across people on my food travels who have never heard of or eaten plantains! For those of you who have never tried them, here is your chance to acquaint your palates with real "yummy-licious-ness." For those of you who are already familiar with fried plantains, add this to your repertoire of simple and swell. Be sure to use plantains with yellow skin, not black; black-skinned ones are too ripe. This recipe is delicious as a snack, but is also served as a dessert in Africa.

SERVES 4 TO 6

3 large, ripe plantains

Corn or vegetable oil, for frying

1/2 cup superfine sugar

1 tablespoon ground cinnamon

2 teaspoons freshly grated nutmeg

1 tablespoon finely grated orange zest

1 cup sour cream

Preheat the oven to 300°F/150°C.

Cut vertically down the length of each plantain, cutting through the skin but not the inside of the plantain. Peel the skin like a coat. Place each plantain on a cutting board, and slice it diagonally into 3/4-inch-thick slices. Place the slices of plantain in a little salted cold water to keep them from discoloring while you prepare the rest.

In a heavy-based, nonstick skillet, heat approximately 3/4 inch of oil. The oil is ready when it starts to ripple with heat.

Drain the plantain slices and dab them dry with paper towels. Gently lower small batches into the hot oil, and fry until the plantains are golden brown on both sides. Remove from the oil using a slotted spoon. Drain on paper towels. Arrange the slices in an ovenproof dish, cover with aluminum foil, and place in the preheated oven to keep warm while cooking the rest.

It is important not to crowd the skillet while frying. It should be easy to turn individual plantain slices over to allow for even browning and so the slices don't disintegrate.

When all the plantain slices are fried and drained of oil, mix together the sugar, cinnamon, and nutmeg. Arrange individual portions of plantain on serving plates, and generously sprinkle each serving with the sugar mixture followed by the orange zest. Serve hot with sour cream.

Potato Dumplings

FUFU

These delicious dumplings are the quintessential starch, often served with Ghanaian soups. In Africa, fufu *is served as one enormous dumpling that families share at mealtime.*

SERVES 4

4 cups boiling water

²/₃ cup potato flour

1 cup cold water

1 packet (6 ounces/180 g) potato flakes

Warm a medium pan with 1 cup of the boiling water. In a small bowl, blend the potato flour with 1 cup of warm water (mix some of the boiling water with part of the cold water; the water must not be too hot, or it will cook the starch) to form a creamy mixture.

Empty the water from the warmed pan. Pour the potato flakes into the pan and add the remaining boiling water, enough to cover the flakes fully. Do not stir.

Using a wooden spoon, stir the potato flour mixture in the bowl and quickly add it to the potato flakes. Speed is of the essence here, as is dexterity! Vigorously stir the 2 mixtures together, pulling the dough in from the center against the inside of the saucepan with one hand and gripping the pan firmly with the other.

When the dough is firm, elastic, and smooth, moisten a small bowl with cold water and scoop the dough into this bowl, either as one large ball or individual balls, and serve.

Cornmeal Dumplings

BANKU

Grains are the staple produce throughout the African continent and are used extensively in African cuisine. Sadly, in some areas little other produce is available. Corn is frequently used to make dumplings, which are used in many kinds of dishes, from soups to meat and poultry. Serve these dumplings with the sauce of your choice.

SERVES 4

6 cups cold water
Salt
3 1/2 cups cornmeal

Pour the water in a medium heavy-based pan or cast-iron pot. Salt the water and bring it to a boil. Transfer half the boiling water to another pot and keep it at a low boil.

Add the cornmeal to the rest of the water in the pan. With a wooden spoon, stir vigorously, pressing against the inside of the pan to eliminate lumps as the dough cooks. Continue to press the dough against the insides of the pan, adding small quantities of the reserved boiling water, until the dough tastes less floury, softens, and cooks through. Remove from the pan and form into balls the size of tennis balls.

Semolina Dumplings

This variation of Cornmeal Dumplings makes dumplings that are a bit coarser in texture, but equally tasty. Serve them with the sauce of your choice.

SERVES 2 TO 4

3¼ cups cold water

Salt

3½ cups semolina flour

Pour the water into a medium heavy-based pan or cast-iron pot. Salt the water and bring it to a boil. Transfer half the boiling water to another pot and keep it at a low boil.

Add the semolina flour to the rest of the water in the pan. Stir vigorously with a wooden spoon, pressing against the inside of the pan to eliminate lumps as the dough cooks.

Keep adding small amounts of the reserved boiling water to make the dumpling soft and easier to knead. Continue to press the dough against the inside of the pan until it tastes less "gritty," softens, and cooks. Remove from the pan and form into balls the size of tennis balls.

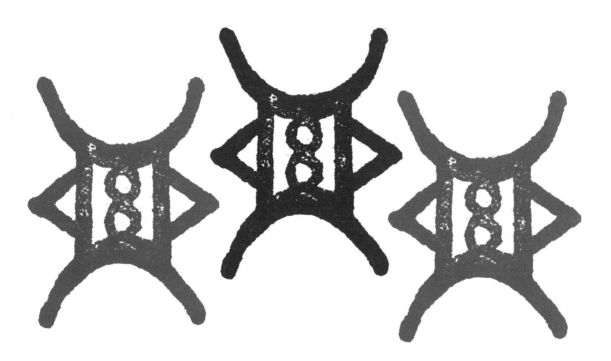

Dorinda's Special Baked Fish

This delicious seafood recipe should be served with homemade Chile Sambal (page 16) and semolina or cornmeal dumplings. This combines three taste sensations: the delicate flavors of succulent fish, crayfish, or crab; the bite of chile, garlic, and ginger; and the balance and earthiness of the dumplings. A typically coastal dish, it is another one eaten with your fingers! In Ghana we have a song called "Komi ke Loo," which is sung with this dish. Komi (pronounced kormi) means "corn dumpling"; ke (pronounced ker) means "with"; and loo *(pronounced low) means "fish" or "meat."*

SERVES 4

4 fresh pompano or
   red snapper

3 tablespoons peeled and
   finely grated fresh ginger

4 cloves garlic, minced

2 fresh red chiles, mashed
   into a pulp

Salt

1 tablespoon butter

1 teaspoon garlic salt

3/4 cup fresh or canned
   crabmeat

4 crayfish tails, cooked
   (optional)

Chile Sambal (page 16)

Semolina Dumplings (page 22)
   or Cornmeal Dumplings
   (page 21)

Preheat the oven to 350°F/180°C. Scale and clean the fish, remove the gills, and cut off the fins and the tails. Lay the fish flat on a chopping board, and make 2 deep but short diagonal cuts in each side, leaving 1/2 inch between the 2 cuts.

Prepare the seasoning by mixing the ginger, garlic, chiles, and salt into a paste, and stuff some in the cuts on both sides of each fish. Rub the rest of the seasoning paste all over the fish.

Rub the butter over 4 pieces of aluminum foil. Place each piece of fish on a piece of foil, and sprinkle a bit of the garlic salt all over each piece. Loosely wrap up the foil to form parcels, and bake for 30 minutes.

Wrap the crabmeat in foil, and warm in the oven for 10 minutes. Unwrap the baked fish and sprinkle the warm crabmeat over each piece.

Serve each person a piece of fish and a crayfish tail, accompanied by Chile Sambal and dumplings.

NOTE: You may choose to cook this dish without the seafood garnish or to use fish fillets instead of whole fish. If you use fish fillets, the seasoning remains the same, but rub it all over the cutlets before baking, rather than inserting it into cuts. Bake fillets for 20 to 25 minutes.

Traditional Fried Fish

With so much of Ghana's fresh food gathered from the ocean, I sometimes think that Ghana-ians should have been born with flippers and fins! Fish is eaten in all possible varieties and combinations in my country, so there is a lot of latitude to play with recipes and come up with your own favorites. The traditional names of this dish are pronounced chinam *or* kaynang. *This is best served hot, garnished with salad vegetables of your choice, such as lettuce, finely chopped spinach, bell peppers, tomatoes, and onions.*

SERVES 4

4 fresh small salmon or snapper

3 tablespoons peeled and finely grated fresh ginger

2 fresh red chiles, mashed into a pulp

1 teaspoon salt

1¼ cups vegetable oil

Scale and clean all the fish, remove the gills, and cut off the fins and the tails. Lay the fish flat on a chopping board, and make 2 deep but short diagonal cuts in each side, leaving ¹/₂ inch between the 2 cuts.

Prepare the seasoning by mixing the ginger, chiles, and salt into a paste, and stuff some in the cuts on both sides of each fish. Rub some of the remaining paste all over the fish.

Heat the oil in a deep skillet, and deep-fry each fish until crisp and golden brown, being careful not to overcook. Remove from the oil and drain.

Serve hot.

NOTE: If you wish, you may grill your fish rather than deep-fry it.

Spinach with Salted Fish

KONTOMIRE NE MOMONE

Kontomire *is the Ashanti word for the large, triangular leaves of the local taro root plant, which in Ghana and other parts of West Africa is called spinach. Because* kontomire *may not be widely available, you can substitute spinach or swiss chard.*

This recipe is a delicious specialty of the Ashanti, and it is often eaten for breakfast accompanied by a combination of baby plantains, yams, or taro root. This dish is very tasty and wholesome!

SERVES 4

1 medium dried salted fish

4 to 8 whole baby plantains, peeled

8 slices taro root, peeled and diced

8 slices yam (or 8 slices potato), peeled and diced

2 bunches fresh spinach or swiss chard, chopped

2 small green onions, minced

4 tomatoes, finely diced

1/4 cup vegetable oil

2 cloves garlic, finely chopped

1 tablespoon turmeric

Soak the fish overnight to remove most of the salt. Rinse, clean, and bone the fish. Shred it into small pieces and set aside.

Boil the plantains, taro root, and yam slices in salted water until tender. Place the uncooked spinach inside a fine-mesh sieve on top of the boiling vegetables to steam very lightly for 5 to 7 minutes.

In Ghana we traditionally mash the spinach, onions, tomatoes, and half the fish in an *aportoryiwa* (pronounced *apor-tor-ye-wa*), a round, earthenware bowl, with an *eta* (pronounced *er-tah*), a flat-ended wooden masher. In a modern kitchen, however, I suggest that you use an electric blender or food processor to blend these ingredients together.

Heat the oil in a small skillet, add the garlic, and lightly fry until it begins to brown. Remove from the heat and stir in the turmeric. (Traditionally, palm oil is used in this recipe, but vegetable oil mixed with turmeric makes a wonderful substitute.)

Place the blended spinach mix in 4 small bowls. Top each portion with 2 teaspoons of the turmeric–garlic-oil mix, and sprinkle with some of the leftover fish.

Decorate each bowl with the boiled vegetables and serve.

The First Independent African Nation

The name Ghana originated under a prosperous and longstanding Sudanese empire that formed part of the pre-European network of trade routes linking the Guinea Coast (West Africa) to North Africa across the Sahara.

After European colonization, Ghana was made up of the former colonies of the Gold Coast, the lands of the Ashanti people, and the Trust Territory of Togoland (now the Republic of Togo). Consequently, Ghana shares traditions and beliefs, culture, and foods with parts of neighboring Togo, the Ivory Coast, and Nigeria.

The present Republic of Ghana came into existence in 1957, when the country became the first African nation south of the Sahara to gain independence.

Chicken Dorinda with Lemon and Herbs

This recipe is one of those you stumble on by accident. When I first arrived in London in 1965, I was young, innocent, and somewhat lost. It was the first time I was really away from home. While I had been at boarding school many times before, this was different. I was actually out of the country, with little chance of getting back home soon. I had finally left home properly and was alone in the big city! I desperately craved some comfort food, flavors I was familiar with, such as Mum's deviled chicken. I couldn't remember the exact ingredients, nor knew where to get them, so I made up my own recipe as closely related to Mum's as possible. This is what I ended up with. Now Mum craves my Chicken Dorinda!

SERVES 4 TO 6

8 to 10 chicken drumsticks or chicken wings

MARINADE

2 tablespoons olive oil

2 or 3 teaspoons garlic salt

Juice of 6 to 8 lemons

1 1/2 cups minced mixed fresh herbs, or 3/4 cup mixed dried herbs

1/2 teaspoon salt

1 head romaine lettuce

1/2 cup cherry tomatoes

3 or 4 large mushrooms, cleaned and thinly sliced

1/2 bunch cilantro

1 lemon, cut into wedges, for garnish

6 cups hot cooked long-grain white rice (optional)

Rinse and dry the chicken pieces. To make the marinade, thoroughly mix the olive oil, garlic salt, lemon juice, herbs, and salt in a large bowl. If you are using wings, cut them into mini drumsticks and flat portions. Put chicken pieces into the marinade, and stir well so that all the pieces are well coated. Cover and refrigerate for 12 to 24 hours to marinate thoroughly.

Preheat the oven to 400°F/200°C.

Arrange the chicken pieces and marinade in a large baking dish and bake for 20 minutes. Remove from the oven and pour off the marinade.

Return the chicken to the oven and bake for 20 to 30 minutes, or until well done and browned. As the chicken cooks, turn the pieces regularly so that they brown evenly. The outside of the chicken pieces should be crisp, and the inside soft and moist. Keep a close eye on the baking process.

Separate the lettuce leaves. Wash and dry them and arrange on a large plate. Neatly arrange the cooked chicken pieces on top and garnish with cherry tomatoes, mushroom slices, cilantro sprigs, and lemon wedges. Serve the chicken hot or cold, alone or with the rice.

Cumin Roast Lamb

When I go to the butcher's to buy a leg of lamb for this recipe, I'm frequently tempted to revert to my "home" method of selecting which one to buy. In Ghana I would hold a leg in each hand and jiggle them up and down to work out which had enough meat to feed the family. These days, to avoid embarrassing my children, I can only resort to pointing gamely at the one I think will be enough to feed us—such is progress.

SERVES 4 TO 6

2 pounds (1 kg) leg of lamb with most fat trimmed off

2 large sweet potatoes or yams, peeled or unpeeled

3 floury potatoes (such as russet), peeled or unpeeled

4 or 5 cups hot cooked spinach

4 or 5 cups hot cooked corn kernels

MARINADE

4 tablespoons ground cumin

1 tablespoon garlic salt

5 tablespoons sesame oil

GRAVY

2 teaspoons cornstarch mixed with 2 tablespoons cold water

Thoroughly rinse the leg of lamb under cold water and dry it with paper towels. Lay it in a roasting pan. Make 3 to 4 deep cuts in each side of the lamb.

To make the marinade, combine all the ingredients in a small bowl and mix well. Insert some of it in the cuts of the lamb, and spoon the rest all over the leg of lamb. Cover with aluminum foil and let stand for at least 2 hours. The longer the meat stands, the stronger the flavor will be.

Preheat the oven to 425°F/220°C.

Bake for 30 minutes, then lower the heat and bake at 350°F/180°C for another hour, or until the meat is tender and cooked.

Wash all the potatoes, and cut each sweet potato into 3 portions and each potato into 2 portions. Lay the potatoes flat with the white sides up and sprinkle with salt to help brown. Arrange the sweet potatoes and potatoes alongside the meat for the last hour of cooking.

When the meat and potatoes are ready, transfer them to a platter. Prepare the gravy by placing the pan on the stovetop over medium heat and stirring the cornstarch mixture into the juices. Thin as desired with boiling water.

Slice the meat, and serve it with the potatoes, steamed spinach, corn, and gravy.

NOTE: You may choose to stuff all the potatoes with the steamed spinach and corn kernels before serving.

Rum Balls

Kubécake is a sweet sold by street vendors throughout West Africa. It is not actually a cake as its name suggests; rather it is an explosion of two fiery forces—a combination of strong dark rum and ginger, with the balancing sweetness of sugar. In fact, kubécake is a version of what Europeans commonly call "rum balls."

SERVES 4 TO 10
(DEPENDING ON
SWEET TOOTHS!)

8 cups shredded dried coconut or finely grated fresh coconut

3/4 cup peeled and finely grated fresh ginger (or to taste)

1 cup dark rum (or to taste)

1 1/4 cups superfine sugar

Preheat the oven to 200°F/120°C.

In an ovenproof dish, mix the coconut and ginger with a generous amount of the rum. Keep it warm in the oven.

Melt the sugar in a large, heavy-based pan on medium to low heat. When the sugar starts to brown at the edges, stir it with a wooden spoon until smooth.

When the sugar is brown (not light brown, not dark brown, but brown), quickly add the coconut-rum mixture. The timing here is critical. The mixture may bubble, but just stir vigorously until the sugar is well blended with all the ingredients. Remove from the heat and cool for about 30 minutes. Moisten your hands with cold water and form into small balls about the size of a Ping-Pong ball.

Serve immediately or refrigerate and serve later.

NOTE: The trickiest part in making this recipe is the timing of the sugar temperature during browning, so stay close and keep a critical eye on the process.

Drunken Oranges

Eating after-dinner desserts is not part of traditional eating customs in most parts of Africa, and access to chilled fresh cream and dairy products is difficult. So I suggest that when introducing desserts to the African dinner table, use local fruits and keep it simple, with one eye on the health aspects. Easy does it! If you prefer not to use alcohol, follow the alternative directions below for "sober" oranges. These oranges are also delicious served with Chocolate Pot (page 159).

SERVES 4

4 to 6 large navel oranges

1 cup mango liqueur, Cointreau, Triple Sec, or other fruit liqueur (optional)

1/4 teaspoon freshly grated nutmeg

2 tablespoons superfine sugar

MINT WHIPPED CREAM

1 small bunch fresh mint

1/4 cup water

1 1/4 cups heavy cream

2 tablespoons superfine sugar

Finely grate 2 teaspoons zest from an orange and reserve. Peel all the oranges, removing the peel and pith carefully to expose the bare fruit. Slice the fruit into thin rounds. Carefully remove any seeds without disturbing the shape of the slices.

Arrange the orange rounds in an attractive, wide, medium-deep serving dish. Pour the liqueur evenly over the arranged fruit, sprinkle with the orange zest, nutmeg, and sugar. Cover and store in the refrigerator for a minimum of 4 hours. (The longer you marinate the fruit, the better it tastes.)

If you prefer "sober" oranges, blend together 1 cup chilled water with the flesh of 3 to 4 very ripe mangoes (or mango pulp and pitted, peeled peaches in equal proportions), and pour the mixture over the oranges. Alternatively, use juice from 3 oranges and 1 lemon or 2 limes, and adjust the sugar content according to personal taste.

To make the mint whipped cream, place the mint and water in a small pan over medium heat. Bring to a boil and simmer until the water is slightly reduced. Take the pan off the heat and allow the mint to infuse the water as it cools. Once the mixture has cooled, remove the mint and mix the infused water with the cream and sugar. Whip the cream mixture until soft peaks forms.

Serve the chilled oranges topped with the whipped cream.

NOTE: For an alternative presentation, do not peel the oranges. Cut the tops off and scoop the fruit from the insides of the oranges. Save the contents and remove the seeds and any pith. In a blender, blend the 2 teaspoons grated zest, nutmeg, 2 tablespoons sugar, and cream with the orange contents to form a thick, creamy mixture; do not use the alcohol. Pour the mixture back into the orange cases. Cover with the orange tops as lids and chill in the freezer overnight. Remove and let sit at room temperature about 2 hours before serving.

IVORY COAST

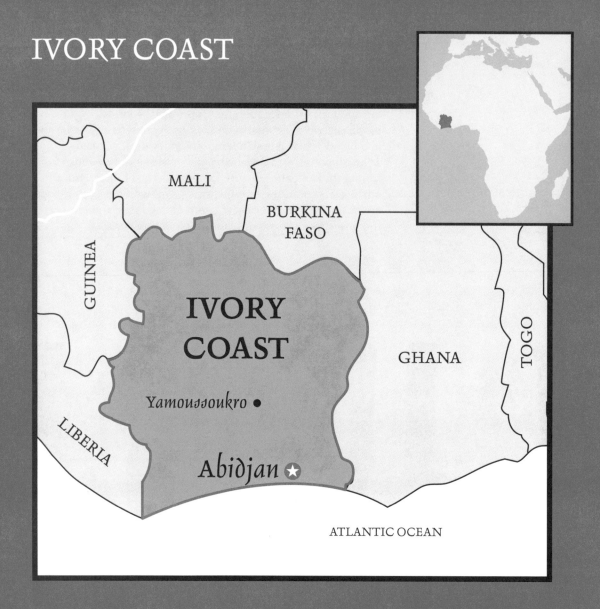

MALI

BURKINA
FASO

GUINEA

IVORY
COAST

GHANA

TOGO

Yamoussoukro •

Abidjan ☆

LIBERIA

ATLANTIC OCEAN

OFFICIAL TITLE: Republic of Ivory Coast (Côte d' Ivoire)

CAPITAL CITY: Yamoussoukro (political capital); Abidjan (economic center)

OFFICIAL LANGUAGE: French

CURRENCY: CFA franc = 100 centimes

CASH CROPS FOR EXPORT: Cocoa, coffee, sugar, bananas, pineapples, cotton, rubber, coconut palm, palm oil, tobacco, mahogany, and vegetable oil

FOOD CROPS: Rice, corn, millet, sorghum, cassava, yams, plantains, and sweet potatoes

TOTAL LAND AREA: 123,939 square miles

Palmnut Soup
34

West African Chicken
Stew with Rice
35

Rice and Offal Balls
37

Plantain Bread
38

Giant Crab Thermidor
39

Fried Smoked Fish with
Gari and Vegetables
41

Savory Ivorian Chicken
and Vegetables
42

Cold Guinea Fowl
43

Mango Fool
45

Palmnut Soup

Traditionally, palmnut pulp is extracted by pounding the fleshy exterior of the palmnut, but for the Western kitchen, canned palmnut pulp must suffice. Luckily, it tastes just as good as fresh and is available in most large cities. The palm from which the nuts are gathered grows in many tropical areas, from West Africa to Malaysia, New Guinea, Fiji, and Brazil. This combination dish is common to West Africa.

SERVES 4 TO 6

2 giant crabs, cooked whole in salted water, drained, and cut in half (remove legs but not the claws—save cooked legs to be added separately to the soup)

1/2 cup cold water

2 pounds (1 kg) lean lamb shanks or chops, or shoulder of beef, cut into chunks

1 salted pig's foot, jointed and cleaned (optional)

Salt

Freshly ground black pepper

2 large yellow onions, minced

3 large tomatoes, blanched, peeled, and puréed

1 1/2 pounds (750 g) palmnut pulp

1 cup boiling water

2 to 3 fresh red chile peppers, ground, or 2 whole habanero chiles (optional)

4 large mushrooms, cleaned

2 pounds (1 kg) fish fillets or cutlets, smoked, grilled, deep-fried, or sundried

Potato Dumplings (page 20)

Remove the stomach flaps on the underside of the crabs and then cut them in half, from top to bottom.

Place the water, the meat, and the pig's foot in a very large, heavy-based pan (not a crockpot, because the initial cooking process requires fairly high heat, which a crockpot does not provide). Season with salt and pepper. Stir in the onions and cook "dry" on high heat, stirring continuously, until the outside of the meat is sealed and browned on all sides. Add the tomatoes, reduce heat, and continue to simmer for 10 to 15 minutes.

In a large bowl, combine the palmnut pulp with the boiling water, beating with a wooden spoon to form a creamy, smooth consistency. Add this to the meat mixture, as well as the ground chiles, mushrooms, and crabs. Simmer on medium heat for 40 minutes to 1 hour, stirring only occasionally to keep food from sticking to the bottom of the pan.

Prepare your choice of fish by removing any residual bones. Add the fish to the soup, either whole or in chunks, during the last 20 minutes of cooking to prevent the fish from breaking up too much and becoming mushy. Once you add all the ingredients, continue to simmer slowly until the meat is tender.

Serve hot with the dumplings.

NOTE: To make palmnut stew, simmer the soup 10 to 15 minutes longer, until it thickens. Serve the stew hot, with *gari* (page 221) or rice.

West African Chicken Stew with Rice

This is a typical West African dish and a popular favorite, so much so that it is rare to attend a major function at which chicken stew and rice is not served. However, since discovering couscous from northern Africa, I have substituted it for rice on many occasions with the same devastatingly delicious effect!

SERVES 4 TO 6

8 to 10 chicken drumsticks

Vegetable oil for frying

Corn flour, for dredging

CHICKEN SEASONING

1 tablespoon peeled and finely grated fresh ginger

3 tablespoons sweet paprika

1 tablespoon garlic salt

4 tablespoons cornstarch

STEW

2/3 cup oil from frying chicken

3 large yellow or red onions, minced

8 green onions, thinly sliced

3 cloves garlic, peeled and minced

1 tablespoon peeled and grated fresh ginger

1 green bell pepper, seeded and minced

3 to 4 hot chiles, seeded and minced

4 tomatoes, blanched, peeled, and puréed or 1 13-ounce (410-g) can Italian peeled tomatoes, undrained and puréed

1 tablespoon tomato paste

1/4 pound (125 g) button mushrooms, cleaned and thinly sliced

3 tablespoons fresh or frozen corn

2 cups chicken stock

3 tablespoons chopped cilantro, for garnish

6 cups hot cooked long-grain rice or couscous, as accompaniment

Lettuce leaves, for garnish

1 or 2 tomatoes, sliced, for garnish

Rinse and dry the chicken pieces. Mix the seasoning ingredients and combine them with the chicken drumsticks. Toss well so each piece of chicken is well coated. Cover and set aside in a cool place for about 4 hours or, preferably, overnight in a refrigerator.

Heat vegetable oil for frying in a large, heavy-based, nonstick, deep skillet. Dredge each seasoned drumstick in cornstarch and fry in the hot oil to seal and quickly brown the outside (about 3 to 4 minutes each). Turn chicken to ensure even browning. When it is golden brown, remove the chicken from the oil and drain on paper towels. Repeat the process with all the chicken pieces. Cover and set aside.

Remove the oil from the heat. Pour off most of the oil, leaving behind approximately ⅔ cup. Return to the heat and add the yellow onions, green onions, garlic, ginger, bell pepper, and chiles. Fry over medium to high heat. Stir regularly and cook for about 15 minutes, or until all the vegetables are soft and brown. Stir in the tomatoes and paste, decrease the heat and continue cooking for 10 minutes before adding the mushrooms, corn, stock, and finally the chicken pieces.

Allow the stew to simmer vigorously for 3 minutes, then lower the heat and simmer gently for about 20 minutes, or until the chicken and vegetables are well cooked and the sauce thickens.

Sprinkle with the cilantro and serve hot with rice, lettuce leaves, and tomato slices.

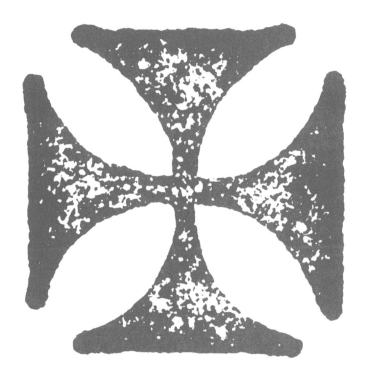

Rice and Offal Balls

I realize some people can't face the thought of eating any kind of variety meat, so it is just as permissible to use up leftover meat in this recipe. Personally, I think liver and the like are delicious, and this particular dish is not only tasty, nutritious, and inexpensive, but it is also an efficient means of dressing up mutton as lamb! I like to serve these, with fresh greens, as a snack.

SERVES 4

2 cups cold water

1 cup (¹/₂ pound/250 g) long-grain white rice

1 pound (500 g) cooked liver or other variety meats or meat, minced

1 yellow or red onion, minced

1 egg

1 teaspoon garlic powder, or 3 cloves garlic, minced

1 teaspoon garlic salt

1 teaspoon freshly ground white pepper

2 cups whole-wheat bread crumbs

2 eggs, beaten with 1 tablespoon milk

1 cup vegetable oil, for deep-frying

In a pan, bring the water to a boil. Add the rice and stir. Cook over low heat, covered, for 15 to 20 minutes, or until the water is absorbed. Let stand, covered, for 5 minutes, then remove the lid. Once the rice has cooled, combine in a large bowl with the meat, onion, egg, garlic powder, garlic salt, and pepper. Mix well.

Form into small balls (the size of Ping-Pong balls). Roll each ball in the bread crumbs and then the egg-and-milk mixture.

Heat the oil in a small skillet and, when it is hot, fry the balls until they are cooked inside and golden on the outside (check the first one cooked). Drain and serve.

Plantain Bread

Plantain is the name of the larger, green, and floury fruit of the banana family, which is one of the most prolific of all carbohydrate-producing crops. It has been calculated that an acre of ground capable of producing 50 pounds of wheat, or 100 pounds of potatoes, can yield as much as 4,000 pounds of plantains! The plantain is extremely versatile and is eaten in sweet and savory dishes.

SERVES 4

3 large, very ripe plantains

2 teaspoons Fresh Chile Sambal (page 16)

1 cup rice flour

Salt

1/4 cup corn oil

2 teaspoons ground turmeric

1 cup salted peanuts, as accompaniment (optional)

Preheat the oven to 350°F/180°C.

Peel the plantains, cut them into small chunks, and put in a large, deep mixing bowl. Mash into a thick paste with your fingers or an electric blender. If you use a blender, you may need to add 2 to 4 tablespoons water for smoother blending.

Add the sambal, rice flour, and salt and mix well. Gently heat the corn oil in a small skillet and add the turmeric. Stir well, remove from the heat, and blend it into the plantain mixture, which should be thick yet soft enough to pour. If it is too soft, add small amounts of rice flour (a tablespoon at a time); if too stiff, add small amounts of water.

Grease a standard loaf pan, and pour the plantain mixture into it. Bake for 1 hour, or until cooked and firm. Remove from the oven and let stand for 15 to 20 minutes before turning it out on a wire rack.

Slice and serve with salted peanuts or as an accompaniment to other dishes.

Giant Crab Thermidor

When crabs are in season, the ones caught on the Ivory Coast always seem to be the biggest! This is my interpretation of a delicious Ivorian equivalent to lobster thermidor.

My first experience of how painful a crab bite can be was when I was ten years old and helping my grandmother to prepare this dish. She had a seaside kitchen from which it was easy to gather live crabs that had been caught in the traditional woven baskets known as flortor. *Luckily, it is now possible to buy cooked crabmeat from supermarkets and fishmongers—and so avoid the nips!*

SERVES 4 TO 6

¼ cup vegetable oil

3 green onions, minced

1 large green bell pepper, seeded and minced

1 tablespoon peeled and grated fresh ginger

6 cloves garlic, minced

2 fresh red chiles, minced

1 tomato, minced

1 tablespoon tomato paste

¼ cup dried shrimp, ground to a powder

1½ pounds (750 g) cooked crabmeat

Salt

Freshly ground black pepper

8 to 12 empty crab shells (ask your fishmonger)

½ cup *ablémamu* (page 13)

Cilantro sprigs, for garnish

Preheat the oven to 425°F/220°C.

In a medium pan, heat the oil and sauté the green onions, bell pepper, ginger, garlic, chiles, and tomato for about 10 minutes, stirring constantly. Add the tomato paste and shrimp powder. Mix well and cook on low heat for 5 minutes. Add the crabmeat and stir well. Taste the mixture and, if necessary, season with salt and pepper. Be careful; shrimp powder can be very salty.

Fill each crab shell with the mixture, then sprinkle the top of each shell with the *ablémamu*. Bake for 3 to 4 minutes, or until the tops brown a little, but be careful not to burn them.

Serve hot, straight out of the oven, garnished with cilantro and a pinch of black pepper.

Cassava

Cassava is a staple of the diet of many African nations, as well as of Brazil, the West Indies, and other countries to which the African people have spread.

Grown for its edible, tuberous roots, which provide a nutritious starch, cassava may be cooked whole or pounded to pulp for use in a variety of dishes. One of the most widespread and productive forms of cassava is as a granular powder of varying consistency. Most popular when it is coarsely ground, this powder is known as *gari* in West Africa, *farinhe de mandioca* (manioc is another English name for cassava) in Portuguese-speaking black areas, and *farine de manioc* in French-speaking black areas.

Whether it is known as *gari* or *farinhe de mandioca*, cassava powder is a superb and nutritious thickening agent for soups and stews. You may also prepare the granules to eat as an accompaniment to other dishes, taking the place of rice or couscous.

Gari

To prepare cassava for use as an accompaniment, put 3/4 cup *gari* in a bowl and add enough lightly salted cold water to cover it completely. Let it stand for 10 minutes, or until the *gari* absorbs the liquid and swells (like rice, *gari* will swell to about twice its original size). Fluff the *gari* with a fork and serve it with a hot dish, preferably with a sauce.

Fried Smoked Fish with Gari and Vegetables

ATSIEKE

Pronounced acherker, atsieke *is street food at its best. Particularly popular at the street stalls and roadside cafes of the colorful Abidjan (the country's economic center) suburb of Treichville,* atsieke *is a combination of fish, vegtables, and* gari, *and is usually served with Chile Sambal (page 16) or Pepper Sauce (page 143). You can also serve it with a combination meat and vegetable sauce.*

SERVES 4

1 pound (500 g) smoked
    herring or mackerel

Salt

3 tablespoons peeled and
    finely grated ginger

1/2 cup vegetable or peanut oil

2 yellow onions, minced

4 ripe tomatoes, blanched,
    peeled, and puréed

1 tablespoon tomato paste
    blended with 1/4 cup water

2 fresh red chiles, minced

1/2 pound (250 g) green beans,
    chopped

1/2 teaspoon garlic salt

2 cups *gari* (page 221)

Season the fish with salt and ginger. Heat the oil in a heavy-based pan, and sauté the fish until crisp and brown. Remove from the oil, drain, set aside, and keep hot.

In the remaining hot oil, add the onions and sauté until they are almost brown. Add the tomatoes, tomato paste, chiles, green beans, and garlic salt. Return the fish to the pan, cover, and simmer for 10 to 15 minutes, or until the sauce thickens.

Put the gari in a bowl and add enough lightly salted cold water just to cover it completely. Let stand for 10 minutes, or until the *gari* absorbs the liquid and swells. Fluff the *gari* with a fork. Accompany each serving of fried fish with some of the vegetables, and *gari.*

Savory Ivorian Chicken and Vegetables

KEJENOU

This is a treasured Ivorian dish, made with chicken and vegetables cooked together, traditionally in an earthenware pot. Pronounced kay-jay-nu, *it is a recipe for special occasions.*

SERVES 4

4 chicken pieces, rinsed and patted dry

6 large shrimp, peeled and deveined, with tails intact

2 teaspoons garlic salt and 2 teaspoons sweet paprika, mixed together

1/2 cup peanut oil

2 yellow onions, minced

4 cloves garlic, minced

4 ripe tomatoes, blanched, peeled, and puréed

1 tablespoon tomato paste blended with 1/2 cup water

2 fresh red chiles, minced

1 teaspoon ground cinnamon

1 teaspoon freshly grated nutmeg

1 teaspoon saffron powder

3/4 cup long-grain white rice

4 to 6 cups chicken stock or equal quantities sweet white wine and chicken stock

Parsley sprigs, for garnish

Butter, for garnish

4 romaine lettuce leaves

Season the chicken and shrimp with garlic salt and paprika, and let sit for 2 to 4 hours in the refrigerator. In a large skillet, heat the oil and sauté the chicken and shrimp. Remove the shrimp when they turn pink and the chicken when it is browned on all sides. Set both aside.

Add the onions and garlic to the same oil, and sauté until the onions start to brown; then stir in the tomatoes, tomato paste, chiles, cinnamon, nutmeg, and saffron. Simmer for 5 minutes on medium heat, then add the chicken, rice, and 2 cups of the chicken stock. Taste and season.

Cover the skillet and simmer on low heat, stirring periodically to avoid sticking or burning. Add the remaining stock as necessary until the rice is soft and the meat is cooked and moist. (This dish is not meant to be dry.) When cooked, transfer to individual bowls, and garnish each portion with parsley and a small amount of butter, and the shrimp.

Serve hot with a lettuce leaf covering each serving.

Cold Guinea Fowl

In some areas of Africa, guinea fowl are more common than chickens. Frequently, they are free-range birds and their meat is darker and tastes stronger than chicken. This is a particularly tangy and aromatic recipe due to the blend of citrus juices and cider, and it is perfect served with a green salad on a hot day.

SERVES 4 TO 6

1 large guinea fowl

Salt

6 cloves garlic

1 tablespoon freshly squeezed orange juice

1 tablespoon freshly squeezed lemon or lime juice

2¼ cups apple juice

2 teaspoons freshly ground black pepper

Chicken stock (optional)

1 tablespoon vegetable oil

Dash of orange extract mixed with a dash of orange oil (found in health food stores)

Pineapple slices, for garnish

Orange slices, for garnish

Season the guinea fowl inside and out with the salt and garlic cloves, leaving some cloves inside the fowl and some embedded in the skin. Put the bird in a large pan. Combine the fruit juices and pepper and pour the mixture over the fowl.

Cover and simmer gently for 1½ to 2 hours, turning from time to time. You may need to add more apple juice or some chicken stock to prevent burning and ensure there is enough fluid to cook the fowl fully.

Preheat the oven to 450°F/240°C.

When the fowl is cooked, remove it from the juices and brush it all over with a mixture of the vegetable oil and the orange essence and oil. Place the fowl in a roasting pan and brown it quickly in the oven. When brown, remove and cool.

Carve the fowl, garnish it with pineapple and orange slices, and serve with a green salad.

Guinea Fowls

Guinea fowl are the most commonly eaten form of poultry in several African countries. Guinea fowl are often caught in the wild, raised in backyards, or sold door-to-door by vendors.

The meat of a guinea fowl is stronger and darker than that of chicken, and the yolks of their eggs are richer and more yellow.

One of the funniest memories I have of Africa is of the commotion as an entire household, young and old alike, would chase an escaped fowl round and round the backyard with assorted native implements in hand to do the bird in!

The Legend of the Crabs

Back in the days when old people's hair didn't turn gray, an orphan called Afua was sent to live with her aunt and uncle. The old couple did not want her, so they would not tell her their names, and refused to give her any protein to eat until she discovered them. They also made Afua perform many household tasks, one of which was to fill a huge drum with water.

Afua often took the drum to the river and wept because she had no way of guessing the old couple's names. Several crabs lived in the riverbed, protected by clay, because in those days crabs had no shells. They heard Afua's distress and decided to help her, for they knew that the old couple would someday walk by the river.

One night the crabs heard the couple call each other by name. The next morning when Afua arrived to fill the drum the crabs excitedly told her. When Afua returned to her aunt and uncle, she was able to call them by their names.

The couple was furious and realized it must have been the crabs who had divulged their secret. In a rage they flung some shell-shaped gourds at the crabs so hard that they lodged on the crabs' backs. In retaliation, the crabs threw gray clay at the old pair, which stuck in their hair.

That is why crabs now have shells—and why old people go gray.

Mango Fool

In Africa, it is common to finish a meal with fruit, and in my mind, mangoes are among the best choices! Many different varieties of mangoes exist in Africa, and during mango season the fruit becomes so plentiful it is hard to know what to do with it all. This delicious recipe is an excellent way to use up a lot of ripe mangoes (and the variation that follows will help you use any unripe ones, too).

SERVES 6–8

4 very large, ripe mangoes, peeled

¼ cup Cointreau, Triple Sec, or other orange liqueur

2 cups heavy cream (amount optional)

Mint sprigs, for garnish

Fresh fruit or glacé fruit, for garnish (optional)

Extract all the mango flesh, including that from the skins and the central seed. Put the flesh in a blender with the Cointreau and cream and blend for 30 to 45 seconds.

Pour into either a large serving bowl or individual dessert glasses. Chill until it sets. Before serving, decorate as desired with sprigs of fresh mint and fresh fruit.

NOTE: A variation of this recipe, Green Mango Fool, uses unripe or semiripe mangoes. Peel the mangoes and slice off all the flesh. Put the flesh in a pot with a small amount of water— 2 tablespoons for every 4 mangoes. Cook the mango flesh until it is soft, and blend it with 3 tablespoons of sugar for every 4 mangoes. Chill and serve with cream.

MALI

OFFICIAL TITLE: Republic of Mali

CAPITAL CITY: Bamako

OFFICIAL LANGUAGE: French

CURRENCY: CFA franc = 100 centimes

CASH CROPS FOR EXPORT: Peanuts, cereals, cotton, fresh fruits, vegetables, livestock, and fish

FOOD CROPS: Millet, peanuts, and sheanuts

TOTAL LAND AREA: 482,242 square miles

Malian Fish Stew

Mali is a landlocked country that has only one fully navigable river, the Niger. So instead of the ocean fish available to their coastal neighbors, Malians eat freshwater fish, such as tilapia, and dried salted fish.

SERVES 4

1 pound (500 g) dried salted fish

4 cups cold water

6 tablespoons vegetable oil

3 large yellow or red onions, minced

2 or 3 fresh red chiles, minced (optional)

4 tomatoes, diced

15 to 20 okra pods, cooked

Potato Dumplings (page 20)

Soak the fish overnight in water to cover. Drain off the water, wash off excess salt, and remove any bones. In a large pan, put the fish and 3 cups of the water. Bring to a boil. Lower the heat and simmer gently.

Heat the oil in a small pan, and fry half the onions and all the chiles until golden. Add the tomatoes and cook for 3 minutes. Stir in the remaining 1 cup water and simmer slowly for about 15 minutes.

Mash the remaining onion with the okra and add to the fish. Stir and simmer for 20 to 30 minutes, or until the fish softens and the water reduces a little. Combine the onion, tomato, and chile mixture with the fish mixture. Serve with the potato dumplings or any other type of dumplings.

The Land of the Hippopotamus

The name *Mali* first appeared some six centuries ago and is thought to have derived from the Mandingo word for hippopotamus.

Chicken and Peanut Stew

MAAFE

Like Palava Sauce (page 15), the origins of maafe *have been lost. Because it tastes so wonderful and is so easy to make, a number of West African countries claim it as their own, each adding a regional stamp to the basic recipe. However, I feel pretty certain that the Bambara people of Mali deserve the credit for this flavorful stew. Rice, potato croquettes, or cooked root vegetables are the perfect accompaniments to this stew.*

SERVES 4 TO 6

1/2 cup peanut oil

3 white or yellow onions, diced

1 whole chicken, cut into serving pieces, rinsed and patted dry

Salt

2 fresh red chiles, minced

4 tomatoes blanched, peeled, and diced

2 tablespoons tomato paste blended with 1/4 cup cold water

6 cups boiling water

1 cup peanut paste or peanut butter

8 okra pods, topped and tailed

2 sweet potatoes or yams, peeled and cut into 2-inch cubes

1 cup corn kernels

4 carrots, peeled and each cut into 4 to 6 chunks

1/4 bunch spinach

1/2 cup sliced parsnips or other firm, root vegetable

1/2 teaspoon ground cinnamon

1/2 teaspoon sweet paprika

Heat the peanut oil in a large, heavy-based pot, and sauté the onions and the chicken pieces (seasoned with salt) until the chicken is sealed and browned. Stir in the chiles, tomatoes, and tomato paste. Blend the boiling water and peanut paste together until the mixture is smooth, and add it to the pot. Stir and simmer for 40 minutes.

Add the okra, sweet potatoes, corn, carrots, spinach, parsnips or other root vegetables, cinnamon, and paprika. Season with some salt. Stir well and simmer gently on low heat until the chicken is cooked, the volume reduced, and the sauce thick.

Serve hot.

Fried Bean Balls

Beans are a common ingredient in the diet of many African people, including those who have moved west to the Caribbean and beyond. The black-eyed variety, from which akara *(or* koosé, *as it is also known) is made, is a versatile and wonderful favorite. This is one of many recipes taken to the West Indies during the slave trade. To this day,* akara *is called* akira *in Jamaica,* accra *in Trinidad and Tobago,* calas *in New Orleans, and* akraje *in Brazil.*

SERVES 4 TO 6

2 cups black-eyed peas

4½ cups cold water

1 to 2 fresh red chiles, finely diced

1 yellow or red onion, finely diced

1 teaspoon salt

2 eggs

6 cups peanut or vegetable oil, for deep-frying

Soak the black-eyed peas overnight in 4 cups of the water.

There are two methods for preparing the beans. If you decide to peel the beans, alternately thresh the soaked beans between your palms and rinse them in water so the skins wash away. Repeat the process until all the beans are skinned and you are left with white beans. If you choose not to peel the beans, simply rinse them several times.

In a blender, purée the beans in small batches, adding the water, ½ cup at a time, to make it easier. Blend the first batch of beans with the chiles, onion, salt, and eggs. When all the beans are puréed, place the thick purée in a bowl, adjust the seasoning, and whisk for 3 to 4 minutes with a hand whisk to aerate the mixture.

Heat peanut oil in a deep skillet until it is very hot. With clean, wet hands, form balls of mixture, gently drop them into the oil, and fry until golden brown, about 5 minutes. Be careful that the oil does not splash your hands. You may prefer to use a long-handled spoon. Fry the balls quickly in batches, and drain them in a fine-mesh sieve lined with paper towels.

Serve hot or cold.

NOTE: These fried bean balls are light and tasty, and the recipe is common throughout West Africa, particularly among Muslims. Fastidious cooks go to the trouble of skinning the beans before mashing them for cooking, but I feel that I lose the quality and color if I do that. It's up to you.

Sweet Millet Fritters

MAASA

Mali is a country in which no food can be wasted. It does not have the bounty of the sea to rely on, and, being an inland nation, it does not have the more temperate climate of some of the coastal fringes. Drought can devastate the grain and vegetable crops that make up a large part of the Malian diet.

Maasa (pronounced mah-sah) are millet fritters, that can be served as a sweet snack or to accompany porridge at breakfast. In Mali, maasa also uses broken rice that is unsuited to other rice dishes. The rice is ground and mixed with the millet flour, sugar, yeast, and oil. The choice of brown rice flour increases the vitamin and fiber content.

MAKES 16 TO 20
FRITTERS

6 tablespoons milk

6 tablespoons cold water

1 tablespoon superfine sugar

2 to 3 teaspoons active dry yeast

2 cups millet flour

2 cups brown rice flour

1 tablespoon baking powder

Vegetable oil, for frying

Confectioners' sugar, for dusting

In a small pan, combine the milk and water and gently heat. Pour the mixture into a mixing bowl and stir in the superfine sugar to dissolve it. Add the yeast and, keeping the mixture warm (for example, on top of a warm oven), let it stand until the yeast becomes frothy.

Sift together the millet flour, rice flour, and baking powder in a large bowl. Stir in the yeast mixture, cover, and let rise for 30 to 40 minutes.

Stir the mixture gently but briefly. It should be the consistency of thick pancake batter. In a large skillet, fry spoonfuls of the mixture in batches in shallow, hot vegetable oil over low heat for 5 minutes, turning frequently to prevent burning and allow the fritters to cook through.

Drain on paper towels and sprinkle with confectioners' sugar. Serve as a snack, a light meal, or, without the sugar, with soups or as a breakfast dish.

Peanut Biscuits

KULIKULI

This tasty and nutritious peanut dish is frequently eaten as a snack or broken into croutons for a salad. Kulikuli (pronounced cooli-cooli*) has an added benefit: it is frequently used in Africa as a treat for teething babies, giving them something to rub against their gums.*

SERVES 4

3½ cups peanut paste or peanut butter
½ cup warm water
Peanut oil, for deep-frying
Salt

Peanuts can often be freshly ground for you at health food stores. Put the peanut paste in a bowl, and use your hand to knead and squeeze the paste to coax out excess oil. Add small amounts of the warm water from time to time to help extract the oil. Continue the kneading and squeezing process until most of the oil is extracted and you get a smooth paste. Season with salt. Add the extracted oil to the oil you will use for deep-frying.

Shape the paste into rings or small, flat biscuits. Heat 1 inch of peanut oil in a skillet and fry the biscuits until golden brown. Remove from the heat, drain, let cool, and store in an airtight container until needed.

Timbuktu: Reality or Myth?

During medieval times Mali was the most important trading area in the Islamic world. It was the seat of ancient empires based on the trade routes across the Sahara, trade routes on which cities such as Djenne, Timbuktu, and Gao built their wealth.

These days *Timbuktu* represents any distant, almost mythical place, but this Malian city was founded in the eleventh century, and at its most prosperous, was a renowned gold trading center and an important educational center for Islamic culture and philosophy.

Jollof Rice

This rice preparation is among the best-known of all West African dishes not only because it is delicious and easy to prepare, but also because the ingredients are readily available in Western countries. Its origin, however, remains a bone of contention among several West African nations. Many regional variations exist—this version is my mother's.

SERVES 4 TO 6

1 pound (500 grams) lean, boneless beef or chicken

Salt

Freshly ground white pepper

Vegetable oil, for frying

4 cups stock, or 4 cups water mixed with 3 crushed bouillon cubes

3 large yellow onions, minced

4 cloves garlic, minced

2 to 3 fresh red chiles, minced

4 large tomatoes, blanched, peeled, and puréed or mashed

3 tablespoons tomato paste

1½ cups diced assorted vegetables (such as carrots, green beans, mushrooms, and bell peppers), mixed together

2½ cups long-grain white rice

Chopped green leaf lettuce, for garnish

Parsley or fresh cilantro, for garnish

3 hard-boiled eggs, for garnish

Cut the beef or chicken into 2-inch cubes or small pieces. Season with salt and pepper. Cover and let stand for 1 to 2 hours.

Heat the vegetable oil in a skillet and fry the meat or chicken pieces until brown. Remove from the oil. Pour the stock into a large, heavy-based pan and add the meat or chicken pieces. Simmer on low heat until the meat begins to soften; remove from the heat.

Drain excess oil from the skillet, leaving enough to fry the onions, garlic, and chiles until golden. Add the tomatoes, tomato paste, half the combined vegetables, and 1 cup stock from the meat mixture. Stir well, adjust the seasoning, and simmer on low heat for 5 to 7 minutes. Add this vegetable sauce to the meat mixture and simmer gently. Stir in the rice. Adjust the seasoning, cover, and simmer on low heat for about 15 minutes.

Arrange the remaining vegetables on top of the rice, and continue to simmer until the rice absorbs all the stock, softens, and cooks and the meat is tender. You may need to add additional water to help the rice cook. If so, use small amounts, totaling up to 1 cup, lightly salted water at a time.

Serve hot, garnished with lettuce, parsley, and hard-boiled eggs.

West African Kebabs

Like plantains and nuts, kyinkyinga *(pronounced* chinchinga*) is street food and a vendor's delight. Because these moist, seasoned skewers of meat and bell peppers attract flies, they are is kept in closed glass cabinets that perch precariously on the vendors' heads.*

The vendors rush into traffic stopped at red lights or up to buses and trucks parked at rest stops to try to make a quick sale. The acrobatics involved in balancing a heavy glass case full of hot kyinkyinga *while simultaneously counting change from a money belt defies description!*

SERVES 4

2 pounds (1 kg) medium-lean steak or liver

3 green bell peppers, seeded and cut into 1-inch squares

1 tablespoon unsalted, dry-roasted peanuts, ground to a powder

SEASONING

4 onions, diced

2 teaspoons peeled and grated fresh ginger

1 tablespoon flour

2 tablespoons unsalted, dry-roasted peanuts, ground to a powder

2 large, very ripe tomatoes, blanched, peeled, and puréed

1 tablespoon garlic salt

1 tablespoon Fresh Chile Sambal (page 16), or Tabasco sauce, or chile paste

Remove any excess fat from the meat, wipe it with a clean damp cloth or paper towel, and cut it into bite-size cubes. Mix all the seasoning ingredients together in a bowl. Combine the meat and half the seasoning and mix thoroughly. Let stand for a minimum of 1 hour before grilling.

Skewer the seasoned meat alternately with the bell peppers, and grill until cooked and browned on both sides. If you use liver, be careful not to overcook it and dry it out.

Remove the skewered meat from the heat, sprinkle with the peanut powder, and serve.

NOTE: You can make any leftover seasoning into a sauce. Simply add 1/4 cup wine (Moselle or ginger wine) and heat it to thicken. Pour over the kebabs. Thin the sauce by adding more wine.

Lemongrass Tea

Herb teas are very popular in West Africa, and this local favorite is poured from long-spouted, ornate, brass teapots into small tea cups with no handles. It is an excellent palate cleanser after a meal.

5 cups cold water

1/2 pound (250 g) lemongrass, cleaned, roots trimmed off, and cut into 2-inch lengths

Sugar (optional)

Bring the water to a boil. Rinse the brass teapot twice with small amounts of the boiling water. Add the lemongrass and pour in the rest of the boiling water.

Allow it to brew for a while, depending on how strong a tea you prefer. Pour the hot tea into small, handleless cups, and serve with or without sugar. It tastes better without milk.

Dishes of Gold

As a trading center, Mali's wealth derived from taxes and custom's duties. The kings of the old empire levied fees on every item that passed through the region.

It is said that the early kings were so rich that King Mansa Musa ruined the value of the Egyptian currency during a visit to Mecca in 1324 because he spent and bartered so much in gold.

Although Mali has been badly affected in recent times by drought and other hardships, what apparent wealth there is appears as gold—much of it worn as jewelry. Malian goldsmiths can fashion exquisite, light, but enormous earrings, which can only be removed by melting down the earpiece. It is said the people of Mali have dishes of gold, but no food to put on them!

MOROCCO

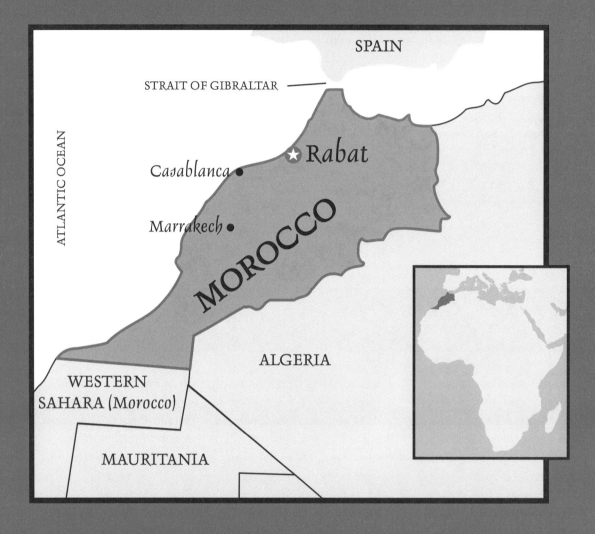

OFFICIAL TITLE: Kingdom of Morocco (known in Arabic as "Al Mamlaka Al Maghrebia")

CAPITAL CITY: Rabat (means "place of faith")

OFFICIAL LANGUAGE: Arabic, although French, Berber, and Spanish are widely spoken

CURRENCY: Moroccan dirham (DH) = 100 centimes

CASH CROPS FOR EXPORT: Sugarcane, beets, cotton and sardines; livestock productivity and crop yields are generally low

FOOD CROPS: Barley, wheat, corn, chickpeas, beans, olives, oil seeds, tomatoes, citrus fruits, potatoes, and other vegetables

TOTAL LAND AREA: 297,685 square miles

Moroccan Lamb Stew with Fruit and Couscous

While Morocco has always held a romantic fascination for adventurous travelers, Moroccan food is just as enticing, particularly the versatile couscous and tagine *dishes with their mixture of sweet spices, fresh vegetables, fruit, meat, chicken, or fish. Paris leads the way, but these days just about every big city can boast its own Moroccan restaurant.*

SERVES 4 TO 6

2 teaspoons ground coriander

2 teaspoons ground cinnamon

2 teaspoons ground ginger

2 teaspoons dried mint leaves, finely crushed by hand

2 pounds (1 kg) lean leg of lamb meat, diced

1¹/₂ teaspoons salt

5 tablespoons vegetable oil

2 large yellow or red onions, minced

2¹/₄ cups vegetable stock or hot water

2 teaspoons saffron threads

¹/₂ cup pitted prunes

³/₄ cup dried apricots

Juice of 1 lemon

Juice of 1 large orange

1¹/₂ tablespoons honey

1 tablespoon preserved lemons, sliced into very thin strips, for garnish

6 fresh mint leaves, or 1 sprig fresh mint, for garnish

4 to 6 cups hot couscous (page 60)

Put the coriander, cinnamon, ginger, and crushed mint leaves in a clean, dry, glass screw-top jar, tighten the cap, and shake vigorously to mix well. Add half of the spices to the diced lamb. Add salt and stir through the lamb to coat and season the meat well. Cover tightly and set aside for about 2 hours, or, preferably, overnight in a refrigerator.

Heat the oil in a medium, heavy-based pan, and fry the onions until they are transparent and soft. Add the seasoned meat and cook on medium heat, stirring often, until the pieces are browned on all sides and the meat juices are reduced by half. Add the stock or hot water.

Dry roast the remaining half of the spices in a small skillet for 1 to 2 minutes on low heat to release the aromas. Add the roasted spices to the meat. Taste and adjust the seasoning. Continue simmering on low heat.

Dry roast the saffron threads in a clean small skillet for 1 to 2 minutes. Be careful not to burn them. Pound or grind the roasted saffron threads into a powder and stir into the stew. Cover and continue simmering on medium to low heat for 30 to 40 minutes. Check and stir occasionally to prevent burning or sticking. Add very small amounts of stock or water if necessary.

Add the prunes, apricots, lemon, and orange juices and the honey. Simmer on low heat for 20 minutes, or until the meat is cooked and tender and the sauce has thickened.

Serve hot with couscous. Garnish with the preserved lemons and fresh mint.

Chermoula with Harissa

This is a delicious Moroccan aromatic fresh herb and spice marinade that you can use for meat or fish. For the best flavor, dry roast your own spices and grind them into powder.

MAKES ABOUT 3 CUPS

HARISSA

6 tablespoons dried red chiles

6 cloves garlic

1/2 cup ground coriander

1/3 cup ground cumin

1/3 cup salt

2/3 cup olive oil

CHERMOULA

1 green onion, white part
    only, grated

3 cloves garlic, crushed

4 tablespoons chopped fresh
    flat-leaf parsley

4 tablespoons chopped fresh
    cilantro

1 tablespoon finely grated
    lemon zest

2 teaspoons ground cumin

2 teaspoons harissa (or more,
    according to personal taste)

1/2 teaspoon saffron powder

1/2 teaspoon salt

1/2 cup olive oil

2 tablespoons freshly
    squeezed lemon juice

When making harissa, it is advisable to wear cook's gloves for protection against the hot chiles. Traditionally, harissa is ground using a mortar and pestle, but you can use a food processor or blender. Clean the chiles by discarding the stems and seeds. Soak the peppers in just enough hot water to cover completely. Let stand for about 1 hour to soften. Drain off the water. Blend together the chiles and garlic, coriander, cumin, and salt into a paste. Very slowly drizzle the oil into the paste while the blade is still running until the mixture becomes a thick, smooth paste. Store in a clean jar in the refrigerator. It will keep for 2 weeks.

Mix together the onion, garlic, parsley, cilantro, lemon zest, cumin, harissa, saffron, salt, olive oil and lemon juice in a mixing bowl. Cover and set aside in the refrigerator for 1 to 2 hours before use.

Couscous

The most well known of the Magreb dishes, couscous is believed to be Berber in origin. Although it is one of the national foods of Morocco, the method of preparation varies widely from region to region, ranging from plain to sweet couscous, with vegetables or meat in between. Couscous is delicious served with toujan *(Moroccan stews), roast dishes, or vegetables.*

Made from durum wheat (semolina), couscous is best prepared in a couscousière, *a specially designed steamer. If you do not own one, a combined pan and steamer works well. This recipe is for cooking loose couscous. Precooked varieties, or* couscous rapide, *are also available at supermarkets and health food stores.*

SERVES 4 TO 6

2¼ cups regular couscous

2 cups cold water

¼ to ½ teaspoon salt

2 teaspoons ground cinnamon

2 tablespoons vegetable oil

1 tablespoon butter

In a large bowl, combine the couscous and water and stir well. Let soak for 10 to 15 minutes. Pour the couscous into a dish towel or a piece of cheesecloth, draining the water and squeezing most of the water from the couscous. Pour the wet couscous onto a tray, fluff out the grains with a fork, cover, and let sit for 15 minutes to swell up. Bring water to a boil in the bottom pan of a double boiler. Tip the couscous into the top pan, spread out the couscous grains as much as possible, place the pan on top of the boiling water, and steam uncovered. If you are serving couscous with a stew, place the couscous over the stew and heat.

Steam the couscous for 20 to 30 minutes, and tip it out onto a wide tray, separate the grains with a fork, and let it cool for 10 minutes. Using your fingers, rub the salt, cinnamon, and oil through the grains to separate them further. Return the couscous to the steamer and steam, partially covered, for 20 to 30 minutes, or until it softens and tastes cooked. Remove the couscous from the steamer and pour it onto the tray again. Stir in the butter and fluff out the grains with 2 forks.

Serve hot.

NOTE: For variety, add cooked chickpeas or raisins to the cooked couscous.

Sweet Couscous

Served in individual portions with milk or cream, this recipe, in which raisins, vanilla or rose water, and sugar are added, is eaten as a dessert in the Magreb countries of North Africa. It is yet another example of the versatility of couscous.

SERVES 4 TO 6

6 cups hot steamed couscous (opposite)

2/3 cup raisins

6 tablespoons superfine sugar

2 tablespoons butter

2 to 4 drops rose water or vanilla extract

1 cup milk or heavy cream

Tropical flowers, for decoration (such as frangipani)

Combine the couscous, raisins, sugar, butter, and rose water in a large bowl and mix thoroughly. Warm the milk in a small pan over low heat without allowing it to boil. If you are using cream, do not heat it.

Place small amounts of the sweet couscous in individual bowls. Top with warm milk or cream, and decorate each serving with a flower to serve.

Fez and Marrakech

Fez, the oldest city of Morocco, and Marrakech, one of the most mystical, are both intriguing walled cities whose narrow, labyrinthine streets are full of long-held secrets waiting to be discovered. Wander along the alleyways and through the archways of the souks, and you will discover all sorts of crafts, jewelry, and exotic, spicy foods for sale. Here tourists, merchants, thieves, and donkeys mingle, and the spectacle—and sounds and smells—are not easily forgotten. Be wary, though, as you can lose your way.

Saffron Rice

Colorful and aromatic, this side dish is perfect to serve with stews and roasts. If saffron is unavailable, substituting turmeric works almost as well. I also recommend using aromatic rices such as basmati or jasmine. Saffron is made of the dried, thin stamens of the crocus flower. Harvesting saffron is extremely labor intensive. Thus, in past centuries, use of saffron reflected great wealth.

SERVES 6 TO 8

6 tablespoons butter

2 cups long-grain white rice

2 green bell peppers, seeded and diced

1 teaspoon saffron threads, or 2 teaspoons ground turmeric

1 teaspoon salt

6 cardamom pods

1 teaspoon hot paprika or cayenne pepper (optional)

4 cups cold water

Melt the butter in a large, heavy-based pan on low to medium heat. Fry the rice and bell peppers, stirring intermittently, for 15 to 20 minutes, or until the rice crisps and starts to brown. Add the saffron, salt, cardamom pods, paprika, and water. Stir well and simmer on low heat for 25 to 30 minutes, until all the water is absorbed and the rice is soft and cooked. You may need to add small amounts of salted water to the rice if it is still hard and uncooked after the allotted time. Fluff the cooked rice with a fork, and remove the cardamom pods.

Serve hot to accompany the stew or roast of your choice.

Moroccan Fish Cousotto

This is virtually a fish risotto, which substitutes couscous for rice with a few modifications, since couscous takes a shorter time to cook. Hence, I have coined a new, fun name for it: cousotto!

SERVES 4

2 tablespoons olive oil

2 red onions, sliced into thin rings

2 tablespoons raisins

3 tablespoons salted, roasted cashew nuts

1 red bell pepper, seeded and sliced into thick rings

1 yellow bell pepper, seeded and sliced into thick rings

1 green bell pepper, seeded and sliced into thick rings

4 fresh, firm, ripe tomatoes, blanched, peeled, seeded, and sliced into thick rounds

1 1/2 cups fish or vegetable stock, or 3/4 cup fortified wine (such as sweet sherry or Madeira) mixed with 3/4 cup water

1 1/2 pounds (750 g) swordfish fillets, cut into 1 1/4-inch cubes

Salt

Freshly ground black pepper

1 tablespoon chopped fresh parsley

COUSCOUS

2 cups quick-cooking couscous

2 cups vegetable stock or water, boiling

2 to 3 teaspoons butter

1/2 teaspoon salt (optional)

Heat half the oil in a large heavy-based skillet and sauté half the onions on medium to high heat for 6 to 8 minutes, or until very dark golden, stirring all the time. Using a slotted spoon, remove the fried onions from the oil, place them on paper towels, and set aside. Fry the raisins in the same hot oil until they plump. Remove with the slotted spoon and add to the fried onions. Fry the cashews for about 1 minute. Remove and add to the raisin-and-onion mix.

Add the remaining oil to the skillet and fry the other half of the onions until golden. Add the bell peppers and continue cooking for about 10 minutes, or until the peppers are soft. Add the tomatoes and the stock, partially cover, and cook for about 10 minutes on medium to low heat.

Stir the fish through the onion and pepper mixture. Taste and season with salt and pepper. Continue simmering for 10 minutes, or until the fish is tender. Do not forget to stir periodically to prevent sticking.

To make the couscous, place the couscous grains in a large, deep dish with a lid. Pour in the boiling stock and stir in the butter and salt. Cover and set aside to keep warm for about 15 minutes so the couscous can absorb the liquid and swell up.

Carefully pour the fish mixture over the couscous and gently fold it through to mix thoroughly into a colorful presentation. Sprinkle with the onion rings, raisins, cashew nuts, and the parsley.

Serve hot immediately.

Salted Fish

Moroccans do not eat much fish, but when they do, it is cooked in a French style and served hot over rice or couscous (page 60).

SERVES 4

2 pounds (1 kg) dried salted fish of choice

¼ cup vegetable oil

1 large yellow or red onion, minced

2 cloves garlic, minced

6 tomatoes, coarsely chopped

1 teaspoon saffron threads

1 teaspoon chile powder or hot paprika (optional)

1 cup cold water

1 green bell pepper, seeded and coarsely chopped

1 red bell pepper, seeded and coarsely chopped

¼ pound green beans, coarsely chopped

Juice of ½ lemon (optional)

Cover the salted fish with water and soak overnight. Drain, then remove the skin, if any, and any bones.

In a large pan, combine the oil, onion, garlic, tomatoes, saffron, chile powder, and water. Bring to a boil on low heat and simmer for 5 minutes. Flake the fish into chunks, and add it to the sauce. Mix together, taking care not to break up the fish pieces too much. Adjust the seasoning.

Add the bell peppers and green beans, and continue simmering on low heat for 10 to 15 minutes, or until the liquid reduces and the vegetables and fish are soft and cooked. Add the lemon juice.

Serve hot.

Pigeon Pie

This combination savory and sweet pie is a specialty of the Fassi (the inhabitants of Fez), although it is believed to have originated in Andalusia in southern Spain.

Traditionally, b'steeya is served as one of several courses at a feast and eaten with the fingers from a communal bowl. The pie is painstaking to prepare, so allow plenty of time— but the result is delicious and impressive.

SERVES 4 TO 6

TOPPING

2 tablespoons vegetable oil

1³/4 cups blanched almonds

1 teaspoon ground cinnamon

1/4 cup firmly packed brown or superfine sugar

FILLING

1/2 cup butter

1 large yellow onion, finely diced

Meat of 3 or 4 squabs, boned and cut into chunks, or skinless, diced meat of 1 whole chicken

1/2 teaspoon ground cinnamon

1/2 teaspoon freshly ground black pepper

1/2 teaspoon hot paprika

1/2 teaspoon ground ginger

1/2 teaspoon ground allspice

1/2 teaspoon saffron threads, or ground turmeric

1¹/2 teaspoons salt

1 bunch cilantro, minced

1 bunch parsley, minced

1¹/2 cups water

6 to 8 eggs, beaten

CRUST

1 cup butter, melted

14 to 16 sheets phyllo pastry

1/2 cup confectioners' sugar mixed with 1/2 teaspoon cinnamon

To make the topping, heat the oil in a large, heavy-based skillet and brown the almonds. Drain the almonds on paper towels, and grind them to a medium coarseness in either a coffee grinder or with a rolling pin and sheets of waxed paper. Combine the ground almonds with the cinnamon and sugar, cover, and set aside.

To make the filling, melt the butter in a heavy-based pan, and fry the onion for 5 to 7 minutes, or until golden brown and soft. Stir in the meat, cinnamon, pepper, paprika, ginger, allspice, saffron, salt, cilantro, parsley, and water. Cover and simmer on low heat for 15 to 20 minutes, or until the meat is well cooked.

Remove the meat from the sauce, which should be reduced to about 1 cup. Set the meat aside. Gradually add the eggs to the sauce, on low heat, stirring continuously until well combined. Stir well, adjust the seasonings, and remove from the heat.

Preheat the oven to 400°F/200°C.

To assemble the pie, lightly grease a deep rectangular baking dish. To make the crust, line the dish with 5 to 6 sheets of phyllo pastry, working from the center outward in a circular, clockwise manner. Brush each pastry sheet with melted butter before overlapping it with the next one. When completed, the pastry should overlap in the middle and overhang the edges of the dish. Lightly brush this pastry lining again with melted butter. Repeat the process for a second, thicker layer of pastry. Brush this, too, with melted butter.

Evenly scoop the spicy sauce into an 10-inch circle of the layered pastry (if there is leftover sauce, reserve for later). Cover this circle of sauce with another pastry sheet, fitting only the inner 10-inch circle by gently tucking the pastry edges under the sauce. Brush the top with melted butter.

Arrange the meat and any leftover sauce on top of this pastry layer. Brush 2 pastry sheets with melted butter and cover the meat, laying them buttered side down. Brush the top with more melted butter. Evenly spread the topping over this pastry. Fold the pastry overhanging the dish inward to cover the almond mix. Place another sheet of pastry on top, buttered side down. Brush the top with more melted butter.

If you have any pastry left, gently lift up the pie and wrap it like a parcel in an overlapping circular manner as in the beginning, tucking the edges under until the pastry sheets meet and the pie is all wrapped up. Brush the pie all over with the remaining melted butter. The pie should now resemble a loaf of bread ready to be baked.

Bake for 20 to 25 minutes, or until the top has browned nicely but the pie is still uncooked. Remove it from the oven, place a larger circular ovenproof dish over the pie, and carefully turn it upside down. Return it to the oven for an additional 20 to 25 minutes to brown the bottom of the pie. Using the same "turning over" process, carefully turn the pie again. Bake for 5 to 10 minutes, which should allow the pie to turn golden brown and cook on the inside.

Remove the pie from the oven and place it on a flat serving dish. Cut 8 thin strips of paper $1/2$ inch wide and 12 inches long. Crisscross these on top of the Bstilla, 4 one way and 4 the other to form diamond shapes. To decorate, put the confectioners' sugar and cinnamon mix in a fine-mesh sieve, and rub it through the holes over the crisscrossed top of the pie. Then carefully lift off the paper strips. The end result should look like a brown-and-white diamond grid and should justify all the effort.

Serve hot. This is a meal fit for a king!

Tagine of Chicken with Prunes

This tagine—*a quintessential Morrocan stew, named for the domed, pyramid-shape dish in which it is served—is made with chicken and prunes, with the spiciness of ginger and coloring of saffron. The recipe is said to be very old—one of the oldest in this region of Africa. Traditionally, it is served with couscous (page 60) and a vegetable of choice.*

SERVES 4 TO 6

6 large chicken pieces

2 yellow onions, 1 finely diced and 1 sliced into thin rings

1 teaspoon saffron threads

1½ teaspoons peeled and grated fresh ginger

Salt

1 cup pitted prunes

4 cups cold water

Combine the chicken, diced onion, saffron, ginger, salt, half the prunes, and the water in a large pan. Cover and simmer gently over low heat. Turn the chicken periodically and stir occasionally. Cook for 1 hour, then arrange the sliced onions on top of the chicken pieces, and the remaining prunes around the chicken. Continue to cook uncovered on low heat for 30 minutes. Add small amounts of water if the original water reduces too quickly before the chicken is cooked. Be careful not to add too much water though, as the sauce should be plentiful but thick.

When the chicken is cooked, the prunes are soft, and the stock is thick, adjust the seasoning. Serve hot.

Tagine of Lamb with Pumpkins, Vegetables, and Fruit

The Sahara forms a kind of culinary barrier as well as a physical one. North of the desert, it is common to use sugar, vinegar, and fruit in savory dishes, an example of European influences. South of the Sahara, however, combining sweet and sour flavors breaches a number of tribal taboos. Ashanti (from Ghana) and Chagga (from Tanzania), for example, believe that eating too much sugary food is effeminate and can even affect their sexual prowess!

Moroccan cooks not only use fruits, but also an enormous range of spices in cooking to give a pungent flavor, aroma, and color to their food. Touajan (the plural of tagine*) are boiled or steamed rather than fried since the Moroccans prefer foods to cook in their own juices.*

SERVES 4 TO 6

2 pounds (1 kg) stewing lamb, coarsely chopped

4 cloves garlic, minced

2 small yellow onions, coarsely chopped

Salt

1 teaspoon cayenne pepper

1/4 cup vegetable oil

1 tablespoon ground turmeric

8 to 10 large tomatoes, blanched, peeled, and diced

1 to 2 red chiles (optional)

1 tablespoon raisins

1 pound pumpkin, peeled and coarsely chopped

2 pounds green beans, halved

Juice of 1/2 lemon

Preheat the oven to 350°F/180°C.

Combine the meat, garlic, onions, salt, cayenne pepper, oil, turmeric, tomatoes, and chiles in a large, deep baking dish. Stir to mix well. Cover and bake for about 45 minutes. Add the raisins and cook for an additional 15 minutes. Stir in the pumpkin, green beans, and lemon juice, cover, and cook for 1 to 1 1/2 hours, or until the meat is tender and cooked.

Serve hot with couscous (page 60) or Saffron Rice (page 62).

Almond Milk

This drink is a Moroccan specialty that is served all over the country as a complement to, or a change from, the Moroccan thé *(tea). It is even available as street food. A delicate combination of almonds and orange makes this a delicious beverage when chilled.*

SERVES 4

¾ cup lightly roasted almonds, finely ground in a coffee grinder

½ cup firmly packed brown or superfine sugar

1 cup water

4 cups milk

1 tablespoon grated orange zest

In a bowl, combine the almonds and the sugar and mix well. Add ½ cup of the water and let soak for 30 minutes.

Put in a blender and blend on low speed as you drizzle in the remaining water. Blend well and let stand for 30 minutes.

Slightly warm the milk and stir in the orange zest. Pour the almond mixture into the milk and pass through a fine-mesh sieve. Stir well and serve immediately, or chill it and serve as a refreshing drink.

The Moroccan Melting Pot

Morocco is the closest country to Europe on the African continent. It is where Arabia, Africa, and Europe merge. The people and culture are an exotic blend of the Berbers (the indigenous people) who live in the mountain villages, the Arab-speaking majority who live in the lowland towns, and a European (mainly French) population. Morocco is a place of great natural beauty, from the soaring Atlas Mountains to the beautiful beaches of the Atlantic and Mediterranean coasts. It is also an area of great historical significance, with the walled city of Fez founded in 808 A.D. The dishes found here reflect a history of centuries of different peoples and their civilizations.

EGYPT

OFFICIAL TITLE: Arab Republic of Egypt (known in Arabic as "Misr")

CAPITAL CITY: Cairo (known in Arabic as "Al Qahirah"), the largest city in Africa and the Middle East

OFFICIAL LANGUAGE: Arabic, although English and French are widely spoken in business

CURRENCY: Egyptian pound = 100 piastres

CASH CROPS FOR EXPORT: Cotton, sugarcane, beets, berseem (Egyptian clover), potatoes, and tomatoes

FOOD CROPS: Corn, sorghum, rice, wheat, beans, and vegetables

TOTAL LAND AREA: 386,102 square miles

Green Soup

Along with the much-loved fuul medames *(page 77),* molohia *is one of Egypt's national dishes. Pronounced* mol-oh-hee-a, *it is a thick green soup, particularly popular with Egyptian Arabs.* Molohia *is the small, green leaf (rather like a small-leafed spinach) of a plant of the mallow family. Substitute spinach leaves if* molohia *is unavailable.*

SERVES 4

1 pound (500 g) *molohia* leaves (available from specialty stores) or spinach

2 pounds (1 kg) boneless red meat or chicken meat, diced

1 large yellow or red onion, finely diced

Salt

Freshly ground black pepper

4¼ cups cold water

2 tablespoons butter

10 cloves garlic, crushed

2 tablespoons ground coriander

2 cups hot boiled long-grain white rice, as accompaniment

1 tablespoon malt vinegar mixed with 1 finely chopped white onion, as accompaniment

Hot pita bread, cut into triangles, as accompaniment

Clean and finely chop the *molohia* leaves (Egyptians usually use a double-handled metal chopper called a *makhrata* to do this) and set aside.

Leaving the fat on the meat, combine it in a large pot with the onion, salt, pepper, and 2 cups of the water. Boil the meat until tender, 30 to 40 minutes, depending on whether you are using red meat or chicken. Remove the meat from the stock and set aside. Add the *molohia* to the stock and boil for about 5 minutes.

Place the butter in a small skillet and briefly fry the garlic and coriander for 1 minute only, without burning. Tip this mixture into the *molohia* and stock while the stock is still boiling. Be very careful; it may splatter, but it smells fantastic.

Serve the soup hot, accompanied by side dishes of the boiled meat, rice, onion-vinegar mix, and pita bread. Allow your guests to make their own selections and combinations.

Okra and Lamb Stew

BAMIA

All my friends treasure this stew—and I can understand why, as it is close to my favorite native Ghanaian dish, Okra Stew (page 12). Increasingly, people use veal and beef in this recipe, but I prefer the tradition and flavor of lamb.

SERVES 4

2 pounds (1 kg) okra

3 yellow or white onions, minced

4 cloves garlic, chopped

6 tablespoons vegetable oil or *samna* (Egyptian rich clarified butter)

3$\frac{1}{3}$ pounds (1.5 kg) bone-in lamb, cubed

Salt

Freshly ground black pepper

2 tomatoes, blanched, peeled, and diced

2 teaspoons tomato paste mixed with 1 cup water

1 tablespoon chopped fresh cilantro

Juice of 1 lemon (optional)

6 cups hot cooked long-grain white rice or couscous (page 60), as accompaniment

Top and tail the okra, and slice into 1/4-inch-thick rings. Do not remove the seeds.

In a large, heavy-based pan, fry the onions and garlic in the oil until they start to brown. Add the lamb and season with salt and pepper. Stir well and cook until the meat starts to brown. Stir in the okra and continue cooking for 10 to 15 minutes on low heat, until the okra begins to soften. Add the tomatoes and the tomato paste blended with water. You may need to add more water later.

Stir well, and simmer slowly for 40 minutes, or until the meat is tender, the vegetables are cooked, and the sauce is thick and creamy. Add the cilantro and the lemon juice, and adjust the seasoning.

Serve hot with rice.

Providing for the Afterlife

For centuries, the wonders of Egypt (the Arab Republic of Egypt) have held great fascination for historians and travelers. Who has not heard of the pyramids, the Sphinx, the bustling city of Cairo, or the lifeblood of Egypt, the Nile?

Many African influences are found in Egyptian culture and lifestyle, and it is now known that the Egyptians sent trade missions as far as the rain forests of the Congo in West Africa during the early Egyptian kingdoms. Some Egyptian food is common to the whole North African and Middle Eastern region. Since the days of the pharaohs, here, as elsewhere in Africa, food played a large part in funerary rites. All over Egypt, tombs of kings, queens, and nobles have been opened to reveal rich provisions for the afterlife—from all kinds of foods to casks of wine and beer.

Fuul Medames

Made from broad, brown fuul medames *beans and* hamine *eggs, this is one of Egypt's old-est dishes, said to date back to the pharaohs. Due to its versatility and great popularity, it has remained one of Egypt's most celebrated national dishes. There are a number of varia-tions on the basic recipe, and it can be used as a dip or spread. Buy* fuul medames *beans at Middle Eastern or Greek delicatessens. You can substitute kidney beans, but the flavor is not as authentic.*

Hamine eggs are hard-boiled, slowly cooked in a juice or stew that lends coloring to the shells and flavor to the whites and yokes. An enduring cultural tradition, it is common prac-tice in Egypt to cook eggs still in their shells in stews.

SERVES 6

3 cups dried *fuul medames* beans or kidney beans, soaked overnight

1 bunch parsley, chopped

Pitted black olives, for garnish

Warmed herb or other bread, as accompaniment

DRESSING

2 or 3 cloves garlic, crushed

2 teaspoons olive oil

Salt

Freshly ground black pepper

Juice of 2 lemons

HAMINE EGGS

6 yellow onion skins

6 white eggs

Rinse the soaked beans 2 or 3 times in water, and place them in a large pan. Boil the beans in fresh water to cover for 2 hours, or until tender. The beans should mash easily when squashed between your fingers, and little or no water should be left when the beans are cooked. You may need to add more boiling water periodically during the cooking process. It is quite common to boil the eggs with the beans, but some people prefer to pressure cook their beans.

Remove the beans from the heat and cool. Partially mash the beans. Mix together the garlic, olive oil, salt, pepper, and lemon juice to form the dressing.

To cook the eggs, combine the onion skins, eggs, and enough water to boil for some time in a medium pan. Bring to a boil on very low heat, and boil until the eggs go brown.

For each serving, spread mashed beans onto the center of a plate. Peel an egg, and stand it in the middle of the bean paste. Top with some garlic dressing and sprinkle some parsley on top. Garnish with black olives. Serve accompa-nied with bread.

Falafel

Egypt, the cradle of civilization, has a cuisine as eclectic and diverse as the cultures living within its borders. I have eaten falafel as long as I can remember, but since seeing it made by a local expert in a restaurant in Cairo and tasting his version, the humble falafel has risen to the top of my regular must-have meals. I like to eat it stuffed into warm flat bread filled with hummus and tabbouleh.

MAKES 16 FALAFEL
BALLS

2¼ cups dried chickpeas or 1 24-ounce (750-g) can chickpeas, drained

4 green onions, chopped

2 cloves garlic, crushed

½ cup chopped fresh flat-leaf parsley

¼ cup chopped fresh mint

½ cup chopped fresh cilantro

¼ teaspoon cayenne pepper

2 teaspoons ground fenugreek seeds

2 teaspoons ground cumin

2 teaspoons ground coriander

½ teaspoon baking powder

1 teaspoon salt

1 heaping tablespoon cornstarch mixed with ¼ cup water

Vegetable oil, for deep-frying

If using dried chickpeas, cover with plenty of cold water and leave overnight. Drain well. If using canned beans, drain and rinse with cold water before use.

Combine the chickpeas, green onions, garlic, parsley, mint, cilantro, cayenne pepper, fenugreek, cumin, coriander, baking powder, salt, and the cornstarch mixture. Process in a food processor in batches for 30 to 40 seconds, or until finely chopped and the mixture is sticky and holds together. Refrigerate, uncovered, for at least 2 hours.

Moisten your hands and press 2 tablespoons of the mixture together in your palm to form into a patty. Fill a deep pan one-third full of vegetable oil, and heat until a cube of bread dropped into the oil browns in 15 seconds.

Test fry one patty to make sure it holds together. It should be firm, but not too hard. If it is too solid and hard, soften the mixture by stirring in small amounts of water, a tablespoon at a time. Form the patties and, in batches, fry for 3 to 4 minutes, or until well browned. Drain on paper towels. Keep the cooked batches in a warm oven until all are cooked and ready to serve.

Serve hot.

Süleyman's Pilaf

Süleyman was a great Ottoman ruler; my Egyptian friend Beatrice named this favorite recipe of hers after him in the belief that a pilaf named this way assures a dish that is rich, exotic, and mysterious. This dish is best accompanied by bowls of plain yogurt, cucumber, sliced tomato and onion, green bell peppers, red chiles, and browned pine nuts (brown quickly in a skillet with a very thin film of oil).

SERVES 4 TO 6

2/3 cup vegetable oil

2 cups long-grain white rice

2 1/4 cups boiling water

Salt

Freshly ground black pepper

1 pound (500 g) mutton or leftover roast meat, cubed

2 white or yellow onions, diced

4 cloves garlic, diced

6 to 7 small tomatoes, blanched, peeled, and diced

1/2 cup raisins

1/2 cup currants

1/2 cup pine nuts

In a large, heavy-based pan, heat 1/2 cup of the oil. When hot, add the rice and stir for 4 to 5 minutes, or until the rice looks transparent. Pour in enough boiling water to cover the rice. Season with salt and pepper, cover, and simmer on low heat for about 20 minutes, being careful not to overcook.

In a separate large pan, heat the remaining oil. Fry the mutton, onions, garlic, tomatoes, raisins, currants, and pine nuts for about 10 minutes, stirring constantly. Season to taste.

Stir this mixture into the rice. (You may need to add some water to help the rice soften.) Cover and simmer on low heat for about 10 minutes, or until the rice and meat are cooked and the rice absorbs all the stock.

Serve hot.

Nesting Pigeons

Egyptians love eating pigeon, and in rural areas of the country, pigeons are specially bred for eating. The tall mud coops are frequently seen on the roofs of their owners' houses. I have added my own variation to this quick lunchtime recipe, which is particularly appetizing when served with a good, chilled white wine.

SERVES 4 TO 6

6 tablespoons olive oil

3 cloves garlic, minced

Salt

6 to 8 squabs, ready for roasting

SALAD NEST

1 head green leaf or romaine lettuce

1 cucumber, sliced

¼ pound (125 g) snow peas

1 cup sunflower sprouts

1 cup afalfa sprouts

2 firm, ripe tomatoes, sliced into rounds

GARLIC SAUCE

4 cloves garlic, diced

2 eggs

1 teaspoon mustard

1¾ cups vegetable oil

Juice of 1 lemon

1 loaf herb bread, warmed

Preheat the oven to 400°F/200°C.

To prepare the squabs, mix the oil with the garlic and salt (for seasoning), and rub over the squabs, inside and out. Arrange the squabs in a large baking dish and bake for about 20 to 25 minutes, or until they are cooked, brown, and crispy skinned. Remove from the oven, drain on a wire rack, and set aside.

To prepare the salad nest, wash the lettuce and separate the leaves. Arrange in a circular manner on a large serving tray. Arrange the cooked birds among the lettuce, add the cucumber slices, snow peas, and sunflower sprouts, trying to camouflage the bodies of the birds so their legs stick out. Sprinkle with the alfalfa sprouts, and give the nest a red border by arranging the slices of tomato around the edge of the serving dish.

To prepare the sauce, put the garlic and eggs in a blender, and blend well on a medium to high speed for about 30 seconds. Lower the setting slightly, add the mustard, and blend again. With the machine running, dribble the oil gently and evenly into the sauce until the mixture is thick and creamy. Blend in the lemon juice. Pour the garlic sauce into a small bowl. (Leftover sauce is a good accompaniment to other poultry, meat, or seafood.)

Serve the nesting pigeons hot or cold with the garlic sauce and warm herb bread.

Birds within Birds

In an old Middle Eastern cookbook belonging to a friend, I once saw a recipe for stuffed camel. The idea was so bizarre and so charmed me that I just had to set about trying to create a manageable equivalent—without the camel! Instead, I use poultry in a gradation of sizes: each bird is stuffed inside another (hence the name!) like Russian dolls. It is an impressive dish and makes a wonderful conversation topic, but it is not at all difficult to make, just time-consuming because of the lengthy preparation of the marinades and the cooking time for the individual birds.

SERVES 8 TO 10

TURKEY

8 to 10 sprigs rosemary

6 tablespoons butter

1 tablespoon garlic salt

1 large turkey

CHICKEN

4 tablespoons ground cumin

1 tablespoon garlic salt

2 teaspoons cayenne pepper

2 teaspoons hot paprika or
    chile powder (optional)

5 tablespoons vegetable oil

1 medium chicken

QUAIL

2 teaspoons tomato paste

1/4 cup cold water

2 tablespoons vegetable oil

2 teaspoons ground ginger

Salt

Freshly ground black pepper

1 quail

1 Saffron Egg (page 85)

POUSSIN

6 prunes or dates, pitted

1 3/4 cups ginger wine, spicy
    mead, or similar

2 tablespoons cold water

1 poussin (baby chicken)

ACCOMPANIMENTS

Roasted potatoes, peeled or
    unpeeled

Baked sweet potatoes, peeled
    or unpeeled

Boiled long-grain rice

Turnips and parsnips, roasted
    with the meat

Steamed broccoli, carrots,
    spinach, or snow peas

It is advisable to prepare and marinate the birds for 12 to 24 hours before cooking for better taste. Also, if you have a big enough oven, try to cook 2 or 3 birds, covered, at once to save time. Cook the turkey first, as it takes the longest, then the chicken. The poussin and quail can cook together.

To prepare the turkey, rub the green spikes off the rosemary sprigs. Put these spikes in a bowl with the butter and garlic salt and blend well. Stuff the rosemary butter under as much of the turkey skin as possible. Rub the rest all over the outside and inside of the turkey. Cover and let stand for at least 12 hours. When ready to cook, preheat the oven to 325°F/160°C, cover with foil, and bake according to weight.

To prepare the chicken, combine the cumin, garlic salt, cayenne pepper, paprika, and oil in a bowl and mix well. Coat the chicken inside and out with this marinade. Cover with foil and bake in a baking dish at 350°F/180°C for approximately 1 hour, or until cooked. Remove from the oven, keep covered, set aside, and keep warm.

To prepare the quail, combine the tomato paste and water to form a creamy mixture. Add the oil, ginger, salt and black pepper to season. Smear this marinade over and inside the quail. Pierce the quail with a sharp skewer so the marinade permeates the flesh. When ready to cook, preheat the oven to 400°F/200°C. Wrap the quail in foil and bake in an oven dish for 15 minutes. Reduce the heat to 350°F/180°C and bake for 20 minutes, or until the quail is tender. Remove from the oven, keep covered, set aside, and keep warm.

To prepare the poussin, soak the prunes in the ginger wine overnight. Mash them to form a paste. Add the water and stir well. Smear this all over the poussin, inside and out. Wrap it in foil and bake in the oven at 350°F/180°C for about 40 minutes, or until cooked. Remove from the heat, keep covered, set aside, and keep warm.

Remove the turkey from the oven. Remove the foil from the quail, poussin, chicken, and the turkey. Stuff the Saffron Egg inside the quail, taking care not to squash either. Stuff the quail inside the spatchcock, stuff both inside the chicken, and finally, stuff the lot inside the turkey, taking care at all stages not to let the birds disintegrate.

Brush the turkey with the pan juices, and return it to the oven without the foil cover. At this point, you can add the vegetables to cook in the juices in the pan. Continue baking at 350°F/180°C for another 20 to 30 minutes.

When everything is cooked, place the "stuffed up" turkey on a large serving dish, and garnish elaborately with vegetables, rice, and flowers and foliage from your garden.

This dish is best eaten in the typical African fashion: do not bother to carve neat little pieces, but just pull off pieces and share around—the idea is that as you get to each layer, a different taste sensation awaits you! Bon appétit.

Meatballs with Tomato and Yogurt

KOFTA WITH TOMATO AND YOGURT

Ground meat, or kofta, *is eaten widely in Egypt and the rest of the Middle East. My mother calls this recipe her simple "pharaoh" dish: "simple" because it is so easy to make and "pharaoh" because it is a dish for kings—and it's Egyptian! Serve these meatballs with rice or couscous (page 60), and steamed spinach.*

SERVES 4 TO 6

1 pound (500 g) lean ground beef or ground lamb

6 cloves garlic, crushed

1 yellow or white onion, diced

1 tablespoon tomato paste

2 eggs

1 tablespoon ground cumin

Salt

Freshly ground black pepper

2 cups vegetable oil

10 to 12 tomatoes, blanched, peeled, and seeded

1/2 cup plain yogurt

4 fresh red chiles, finely chopped

In a deep bowl, combine the meat, garlic, onion, tomato paste, eggs, and cumin, and season with salt and pepper. Mix together thoroughly. Form into small balls the size of Ping-Pong balls.

Heat the vegetable oil in a deep skillet. Fry the meatballs in batches until brown and set aside. Blend or process the tomatoes to a purée. Put the fried meatballs in a large pan, pour the tomato purée over them, stir, and season to taste. Simmer gently for 10 to 15 minutes, or until cooked. Test doneness by cutting open 1 meatball. If it is still pink, the meatballs are not fully cooked.

Serve with bowls of yogurt and the chopped chiles.

Saffron Eggs

Saffron Eggs are cooked using a method similar to the one for hamine eggs (page 77). As a decorative addition to many dishes, hard-boil 4 eggs, then cool in cold water and peel. Put 1/2 teaspoon of saffron threads in a pot filled with hot water, add the eggs, and slowly bring it to a boil. Boil for 5 to 10 minutes, strain, cool, and serve as usual. The eggs absorb the color of the saffron and look very pretty. Birds within Birds (page 81) uses a Saffron Egg as part of the dish.

ETHIOPIA

OFFICIAL TITLE: Federal Democratic Republic of Ethiopia

CAPITAL CITY: Addis Ababa (means "new flower" in Amharic)

OFFICIAL LANGUAGES: Amharic and English

CURRENCY: Ethiopian birr = 100 cents

CASH CROPS FOR EXPORT: Coffee, sugar, and cotton; due to persistent drought and war, production has been severely depleted

FOOD CROPS: Corn, *teff* (local grain), sorghum, millet, wheat, and livestock (all readily available under normal circumstances)

TOTAL LAND AREA: 437,840 square miles

Vegetable Stew

This particular wot, *or stew, is very similar to the peanut stews from other parts of Africa, except it is made with vegetables only.* Shiro Wot *is frequently used in Muslim areas of Ethiopia during periods of religious fasting, when meat, dairy products, and poultry are excluded from the diet. You can, of course, add meat to the recipe if you prefer.*

SERVES 4

2 cups boiling water

1 cup peanut paste or
 peanut butter

4 tablespoons butter

1 yellow onion, diced

2 teaspoons *berbere* (page 91),
 or 2 or 3 fresh red chiles,
 diced

Salt

1 cup sweet corn kernels

1/2 pound (250 g) root and
 green vegetables of choice,
 diced

1/2 pound (250 g) pumpkin or
 cabbage (optional), diced

1 large semiripe plantain or
 banana, peeled and cut
 into 6 rounds

1 tablespoon tomato paste

Ethiopian Flat Bread (page 92)

Blend together the boiling water and peanut paste, and set aside. Melt the butter in a large, heavy-based pan over low heat. Sauté the onions and *berbere* for about 5 minutes. Stir in the blended peanut paste, season with salt, and simmer on low heat, stirring regularly to prevent sticking, for about 30 minutes.

Add the corn, root vegetables, pumpkin, and plantain and simmer for 15 to 20 minutes, until the vegetables are cooked and the sauce has thickened. If using green vegetables, add them only in the last 5 minutes, so they do not overcook.

Serve with Ethiopian Flat Bread (page 92), or alone.

Chicken Stew

Wot (pronounced whot*) is the Ethiopian term for "stew," and* doro wot *is chicken stew made in the Ethiopian style. It is delicious and thick, and it is generally served ceremoniously on the famous Ethiopian Flat Bread. Everyone digs into the stew and accompaniments, tearing off pieces of the bread to soak up even more of the* wot, *which is eaten with the fingers.*

You can substitute red meat for the chicken—the dish is then known as beg wot.

SERVES 4

1/2 cup butter or ghee (Indian cooking butter)

2 large yellow onions, diced

3/4 cup tomato paste

3 cups cold water

2 teaspoons garlic salt

1 teaspoon freshly ground black pepper

2 fresh red chiles, finely diced, or 2 teaspoons *berbere* (page 91)

2 pounds (1 kg) chicken pieces

6 hard-boiled eggs, shelled

Ethiopian Flat Bread (page 92)

Melt the butter in a heavy-based pan and sauté the onions for 10 minutes, or until golden. Mix the tomato paste with 1/2 cup of the water to form a creamy paste. Stir the paste into the onions, along with the garlic salt, pepper, chiles, and the remaining water. Adjust the seasoning and simmer gently on low heat for about 10 minutes.

Prick each chicken piece and egg all over with a skewer or fork, and add them to the simmering sauce. Stir well to ensure the chicken and eggs are well coated in sauce. Simmer on low heat for 30 to 40 minutes, or until the chicken and eggs have absorbed the flavors of the sauce, the chicken is tender, and the sauce has thickened.

Serve hot with flat bread. Set the flat bread as the centerpiece of the meal. Alternatively, do it the Ethiopian way: cover a large serving platter with the bread, place the stew in the center surrounded by an assortment of vegetables, and invite your guests to eat communally by breaking off pieces of bread and scooping up the stew without using cutlery. It gives new meaning to "intimacy"!

Eggplant and Bean Salad

Eggplant is popular all over the north and northeastern regions of Africa. It is a very versatile vegetable and forms the basis of dips and spreads, salads and stews.

Traditional African eggplants are cream colored and smaller than their purple counterparts. Growing, they look just like clusters of eggs hanging on a low shrub. The cream and yellow varieties are most common south of the Sahara.

SERVES 4

3 large eggplants, peeled and diced

Juice of 1 lemon

1 tablespoon salt

¼ cup olive oil

2 cloves garlic, finely diced

Freshly ground black pepper

2 cups cooked beans of choice, cold

2 teaspoons sugar

1 loaf bread, warmed, as accompaniment

Place the diced eggplant in a bowl. Mix the lemon juice with the salt and pour over the eggplants. Let stand for 10 to 15 minutes.

Combine the oil, garlic, beans, and pepper for seasoning in a large salad bowl with the eggplant and marinade. Toss together well, sprinkle with the sugar, and serve with the bread.

Berbere

Many Ethiopian dishes use the seasoning *berbere* (pronounced *bari baray*), which is a combination of ground spices, pepper, and salt. To make a Western version of *berbere* (in the absence of local Ethiopian spices), follow the instructions below.

Mix together 1 teaspoon of each of the following ingredients: ground cumin, ground coriander, ground ginger, ground cardamom, ground fenugreek seeds, freshly grated nutmeg, ground cinnamon, ground cloves, and onion powder.

Toast lightly in a heavy skillet on low heat for 3 to 4 minutes, stirring constantly.

Add $1/4$ teaspoon ground allspice, $1 1/4$ cups cayenne pepper, $1/2$ cup sweet paprika, $1/4$ cup salt, and 2 tablespoons freshly ground black pepper.

Continue toasting on low heat for approximately 10 minutes, stirring constantly. Remove from the heat and cool. This makes about 1 pound. It will last, in an airtight container, for about 1 year.

To make a small quantity of a quick equivalent of *berbere*, use the same cooking method, but the following quantities.

Mix together 1 teaspoon ground ginger, $1/2$ teaspoon ground cinnamon, $1/4$ teaspoon ground dried mint, 6 tablespoons cayenne pepper, and 2 tablespoons sweet paprika. This recipe makes approximately $1/2$ cup.

Ethiopian Flat Bread

Injera *is an Ethiopian flat bread—with a difference. This spongy, thin bread is generally made into large rounds, a few of which when put together can quite easily cover a tabletop. Indeed, on occasions,* injera *is used in place of a tablecloth or table covering. Dishes such as* doro wot *(page 89) are served directly on the* injera *tablecloth for big communal meals. The bread is broken off from around the edges to scoop up the stew. The idea is to eat from the outside in—very original and a lot of fun for a dinner party idea.*

Injera is usually made from an Ethiopian flour called teff *in the Amharic language. Teff is a cereal grain widely grown in Ethiopia for human consumption, but in other countries as fodder. There are two kinds of* teff—*red (which is richer in iron and minerals) and white—and these account for the local differences in the color of* injera. *Teff flour is often not readily available in Western shops, but where there is a will, there will always be a way! Expatriate Ethiopians have evolved different ways of making* injera *outside of Ethiopia. This recipe was given to me by my Ethiopian friend Aggie, who not only invited me to a fantastic evening of feasting at her home, but also insisted on showing me how to make good* injera *in Australia!*

MAKES 18 TO 20 FLAT BREADS

1¹/₂ teaspoons active dry yeast (equals 1 tablespoon fresh yeast)

4¹/₄ cups lukewarm water

2 cups self-rising flour

Soak the yeast in ¹/₄ cup of the lukewarm water and let stand to froth, about 10 minutes. Stir gently to ensure the yeast has dissolved.

Using a large, nonstick skillet, dry roast the flour over low to medium heat, stirring continuously to prevent burning. It takes patience, but it is worth it. It helps the yeast work better and makes the *injera* smell so good!

Roast the flour for about 10 minutes, and tip it into a large bowl. Allow the flour to cool a little, then stir in the yeast mixture and the 4 cups of the lukewarm water. It is important that the temperature of the mix is only lukewarm, or the yeast will die and the *injera* will not work. Use your hand to mix into a smooth batter.

Cover the *injera* batter with a dish towel and set aside for 30 minutes. It is normal for the dough to smell slightly "fermented."

Heat a large, nonstick skillet on medium to high heat. It is important to use an absolutely clean, unblemished skillet to keep the *injera* from sticking. When a drop of water sizzles and immediately evaporates from the skillet, it is ready to cook the *injera*. You do not need any oil. Stir through the "proved" *injera* batter to mix any sediment that has gathered at the bottom of the bowl while the batter was "proving." Scoop a medium-size soup ladle of the batter, and gently pour it into the hot pan skillet. Swirl the batter gently in the skillet to cover totally the base, like a pancake batter.

Decrease the heat to medium and gently cook the *injera*. Allow it to firm similar to a pancake. Unlike a pancake, however, *injera* does not need to be tossed or turned. Instead, use a spatula to gently lift the edges as they firm up to check the state of readiness. Cook each *injera* for 5 to 7 minutes, or until the *injera* cooks and sets and the color ranges between ivory and very pale caramel. The consistency should be lacy, chewy soft, and pliable. Carefully lift out the cooked *injera* and place it on a flat tray lined with waxed paper.

Wipe the skillet clean with a damp cloth, reheat it, and continue the cooking process with the remaining batter until almost all the *injera* is made. Place sheets of waxed paper between the rounds of *injera* as they are made, to separate and keep them from sticking together. Save a ladle of uncooked batter for the next batch (see Note).

Serve immediately. *Injera* is usually eaten with stews.

NOTE: It is common practice to leave about a cup or ladle of the old batter in the bowl to form the basis of the next batch of batter. That way, you need not add any more yeast to future *injera* batter. Just dry roast 2 cups self-rising flour, as described above, add the flour and 4 cups lukewarm water to the leftover batter, allow it to prove, and you're ready.

Ethiopian Fish

Many of the dishes I have included from Ethiopia use a local seasoning called berbere *(pronounced* bari-baray*), a combination of dry, hot spices frequently used in stews. The combination of salted fish and* berbere *makes this simple dish delicious.*

SERVES 4

4 salted fish

4 cloves garlic, crushed

2 teaspoons *berbere* (page 91)

4 large tomatoes, sliced

8 teaspoons peanut oil

Ground peanuts, for sprinkling (optional)

Ethiopian Flat Bread (page 92), as accompaniment

Soak the salted fish in water overnight to remove excess salt.

Preheat the oven to 425°F/220°C. Rinse the fish well and soak for 10 minutes in a bowl of boiling water. Lightly grease a large baking dish, carefully lift out each fish, and place it in the dish.

Sprinkle some crushed garlic and 1/2 teaspoon of *berbere* on each fish. Arrange slices from 1 tomato down the length of the fish and then sprinkle with 2 teaspoons of the peanut oil and some peanuts.

Cover and bake for about 30 minutes, or until the fish is tender and cooked through.

Serve hot on top of individual portions of flat bread.

NOTE: You may choose to season each fish on greased aluminum foil, wrap it up, and bake as above; the cooking time will be 15 to 20 minutes.

Spicy Raw Beef

Generally, Africans prefer their meat well cooked (sometimes too well cooked), so this Ethiopian raw meat dish is quite unusual. In fact, it reminds me of a Japanese recipe that a friend gave me years ago.

Ethiopians add a local yellow pepper called mitmita *to the meat, believing that the hot pepper will kill any germs. Because this variety of pepper is not available everywhere, I suggest using any variety of moist, coarsely grated prepared chile sauce.*

SERVES 4 TO 6

1 pound (500 g) lean ground beef

1 white onion, diced

1/4 cup vegetable oil

Juice of 1 lemon, or 1/4 cup wine or cider vinegar (optional)

2 to 4 teaspoons red chile sauce

Salt

Freshly grated black pepper

1 teaspoon ground cumin

1 teaspoon ground cinnamon

1 teaspoon ground coriander

1 teaspoon minced garlic

Assortment of green salad vegetables (such as lettuce, alfalfa sprouts, sunflower sprouts, green bell peppers, and so on)

Put the beef, onion, oil, lemon juice, chile sauce, salt, pepper, cumin, cinnamon, coriander, and garlic in a bowl and mix together thoroughly. Form into small balls or flat patties. Arrange the salad on individual plates with the meat in the middle. Garnish as you wish and serve cold.

NOTE: I have personally never been able to eat raw meat, so I lightly cook my portion in the microwave for a few seconds, then break up the meat with a fork, and sprinkle it over my salad.

Ethiopia

An arid land of mountainous plateaus with serious erosion and drought problems, Ethiopia is also a country of great beauty and interest to the traveler prepared to work a bit harder to get off the beaten track. The intrepid traveler should look beyond the bureaucratic difficulties to the majesty of the rock-hewn churches of Lalibela and the beautiful Rift Valley lakes, and perhaps sample transportation by mule in one of the mountainous regions of this country, which is slowly opening up, after being cut off from the rest of the world for many years.

The Chosen Ones

A persistent belief in Ethiopia that Ethiopians are the chosen people of God stems from a long-held creation legend. According to this legend, God molded the first humans from clay. He put the first batch in an oven to bake, but left them there too long, and they emerged burned and black, so he threw them away to the southern part of Africa. He took the second batch from the oven too soon, and they were pasty and white, so he threw them northward, where they became the Arab and European populations. The third and final batch was just right, and God put them in Ethiopia.

Spiced Aromatic Beef

ABISH

The African tradition is to use meat as a flavoring or condiment and rarely as the main component of a meal; this simple meat dish is excellent as a stuffing for fruits and vegetables, such as green, unripe papaya, green bell peppers, or baked potatoes.

Ideally, this dish should be cooked completely in butter, but because butter is expensive in much of Africa, most people use just a tablespoon and season it with the herb of their choice.

SERVES 4

½ cup butter or vegetable oil

1 large yellow onion, diced

1 tablespoon peeled and grated fresh ginger

1 tablespoon minced garlic

2 tomatoes, diced

1 pound (500 g) lean ground beef

Salt

2 to 3 eggs, beaten

1 tablespoon ground turmeric

1 tablespoon butter mixed with 1 tablespoon minced fresh parsley

Parsley sprigs, for garnish

1½ cups grated aged goat cheese (optional)

Heat the butter in a large pan and sauté the onion until golden. Stir in the ginger, garlic, tomatoes, and beef; season with salt. Cook on low heat for 15 to 20 minutes, stirring regularly to prevent burning. Combine the eggs with the mixture in the pan, and cook for 10 minutes. Remove from the heat. Mix in the turmeric and seasoned butter, and top with the parsley and cheese.

Serve alone or with rice or fresh bread; mix with steamed corn; or use the beef to stuff other vegetables.

KENYA

OFFICIAL TITLE: Republic of Kenya (known in Kiswahili as "Djumhuri ya Kenya")

CAPITAL CITY: Nairobi (means "swamp")

OFFICIAL LANGUAGE: Kiswahili and English, although Kikuyu, Luo, Kikamba and Kiluhya are widely spoken

CURRENCY: Kenyan shilling (KS) = 100 cents

CASH CROPS FOR EXPORT: Tea, coffee, sugar, cotton, pyrethrum, wattle, sisal, and pineapples

FOOD CROPS: Corn, sorghum, cassava, beans, vegetables, fruits, livestock, and fish

TOTAL LAND AREA: 224,943 square miles

Leftovers Stew

SUKUMA WIKI

This meat and vegetable recipe was given to me by Mike and Jenny Piper. Mike, who speaks impeccable Kiswahili, told me that sukuma wiki *(pronounced* su kuma wi-kee*) is Kiswahili and literally translates as "push the weak." The stew is frequently served the day before payday, when all that one might have in the kitchen is leftovers. I might add, however, that it is also available at most restaurants in Kenya—even at Nairobi's finest—on almost every day of the week. I like to eat this dish with* ugali *(page 113), boiled rice, and plantains or bananas.*

SERVES 4

½ pound (250 g) leftover meat, cooked or raw, chopped into bite-size pieces

6 tablespoons vegetable oil

2 yellow or red onions, diced

4 tomatoes, blanched, peeled, and quartered

1 green bell pepper

Salt

Freshly ground black pepper

1 bunch spinach, chopped

If you are using raw meat, start by frying the meat lightly in a large pan with hot oil. When the meat is nearly cooked, add the onions and cook until they are soft and translucent. Add the tomatoes, green pepper, and any precooked meat. Season with salt and pepper and cook until the meat is cooked through.

Stir in the spinach and cook on low heat for about 5 minutes, stirring periodically. Give the whole pan a final stir before serving.

The Maasai

The Maasai, once a powerful and ferocious people, inhabit the open grasslands of the Rift Valley of Kenya. Ignoring the social and political changes that have taken place in that country, they have retained their nomadic ways, herding cattle, sheep, and goats.

Cattle are of prime importance to the Maasai, for they believe the sky god, Enkai, entrusted these beasts to them. Wealth and social status among the Massai is measured by the number of cattle owned. In the arid areas of the Rift Valley, livestock is moved seasonally, driven by the constant quest for water and grazing land.

Because the cattle are of such significance, they are only slaughtered when they grow old and then generally for ceremonial purposes, such as rites of passage. A mainstay of the Maasai diet is milk, which is carried in decorated gourds and may also be mixed with cow's blood. Any meat comes from butchered goats and sheep.

It is also taboo to kill wild game except for buffalo and eland. The Maasai believe it is sacrilege to cultivate the land (and thus disturb the cattle fodder). Like the Ashanti, Mandingos, Fulani (of West Africa), and the Zulus (of southern Africa), the Maasai are a very proud race. They regard Europeans as "people of the paper" and disdain other groups who farm the land and adopt modern methods, calling them "black Europeans."

Corn and Bean Mash

Although some Kenyans find this dish rather dull, I think it is wonderfully versatile. It is like a Kenyan version of fuul medames *(page 77). An innovative cook can make much of* irio, *adding different flavorings such as garlic, fresh herbs, and spices; combining it with dried salted fish, seafood, or minced meat; or stuffing it into various vegetables to bake.*

SERVES 4 TO 6

2 cups dried beans or peas of choice

Salt

1 1/2 cups lentils

2 semiripe plantains or bananas, each peeled and cut into 6 rounds

4 large potatoes, peeled and quartered

2 cups corn kernels

Freshly ground black pepper

4 tablespoons butter

Soak the beans or peas of your choice in enough cold water to cover for 2 hours. Rinse them thoroughly under cold water. Put them in a large pan with water and salt. Bring to a boil and simmer for 15 to 20 minutes.

Add the lentils, plantains, potatoes, corn kernels, and a little more water if necessary. Season with salt and pepper. Bring to a boil and simmer slowly until all the vegetables are soft and cooked. Drain off any excess water.

In a very large bowl, mash all the boiled vegetables and the butter together as smoothly as possible. For variation, you can mash in any spice or herb seasoning, any cooked fish or meat, or even another vegetable such as pumpkin.

Serve alone or as an addition to any meat or fish dish.

Crunchy Bananas

This fruit combination recipe was supplied by my friends Mike and Jenny Piper. N'dizi (pronounced ndee-zi) *is Swahili for "bananas," and the crunchy peanut and banana pieces served with ripe Mango Fool (page 45) and ice cream or a sliver of coconut make a delicious end to a meal.*

SERVES 4 TO 6

1 tablespoon cold water

8 bananas, peeled

1/2 cup butter, melted

1 cup unsalted roasted peanuts, chopped

Preheat the oven to 375°F/190°C.

Put the water in a large pan over medium heat. When the water starts to boil, add the bananas, cover, and steam for 10 seconds, until heated through. Be careful that they do not become too soft. Drain and roll them in the melted butter. Roll each one separately in chopped peanuts.

Arrange them on a baking dish, and bake for 15 minutes, or until the peanuts are lightly browned. Serve hot.

Rift Valleys and Soda Lakes

The rift valleys of East Africa formed along fault lines in the earth's crust. These valleys are created by blocks of the crust dropping down, with surrounding areas of higher ground forming hills and mountain ranges. Mount Kenya and Mount Kilimanjaro (in Tanzania) are peaks created in such a way, and both are actually extinct volcanoes.

Lakes form on the floors of the valleys, caused by runoff from the surrounding slopes. These lakes are frequently shallow and have a high alkaline content created by a combination of high evaporation and volcanic minerals. Such lakes are called soda lakes. Despite the high alkaline levels, many creatures exist in and around the lakes. The main soda lakes in Kenya are Nakuru, Bogoria, and Magadi, and in Tanzania, Lake Natron.

Giriama Fish Curry

GIRIAMA GOURMET

Giriama (pronounced ghe-ree-yah-mah*) is a Kenyan coastal fish dish named after the Giriama people of Malindi. Here, the fish is flavored with garlic, saffron, cumin, turmeric, and coconut milk, in a kind of regional fish curry. This is yet another recipe from my friend and colleague Mike Piper and his wife, Jenny.*

SERVES 4 TO 6

6 cloves garlic, chopped

1 green onion, chopped

1 teaspoon saffron threads

1 teaspoon ground cumin

1 teaspoon ground turmeric

4 tablespoons butter

4 sea bass fillets, ½ pound (250 g) each

Salt

Freshly ground black pepper

4 tomatoes, chopped

3 cups coconut milk

In a large skillet, stir-fry the garlic, onion, saffron, cumin, and turmeric in the butter for about 5 minutes. Stir in the fish pieces and season with salt and pepper. Cook for 10 to 15 minutes. Add the tomatoes and cook for 10 minutes. Stir in the coconut milk and simmer slowly for 15 to 20 minutes, or until the sauce reduces to a creamy texture.

Serve immediately.

NOTE: To serve, the traditional recipe calls for a glowing piece of charcoal to be added before serving, as it is thought to put extra flavor and "real" fire into the sauce. However, only a professional should use charcoal; it is not recommended for the average kitchen! It can be dangerous and also leaves small flakes of charcoal in the sauce.

Chicken in Coconut Milk

There are a variety of coconut and meat dishes from countries surrounded by or bordered by the sea. But this particular chicken and coconut recipe from Kenya, with its overtones of mixed cultural influences, is special to me for its simplicity and because chicken is traditionally served in Africa on special occasions and to celebrate the presence of guests.

Chicken is not as commonplace in Africa as it is in industrialized countries. The birds are caught fresh from the backyard, plucked, and prepared on the same day, lending a distinctive flavor to the dish.

SERVES 4 TO 6

Garlic salt

1/2 cup vegetable oil

1 whole chicken, cut into
   6 to 8 serving pieces

2 yellow onions, chopped

2 cloves garlic, chopped

4 large tomatoes, blanched,
   peeled, seeded, and diced

Salt

Freshly ground black pepper

2 cups coconut milk

1 bunch cilantro

Rub the garlic salt and about 1/4 cup of the oil all over the chicken pieces. Arrange the pieces on a charcoal grill and lightly brown or, alternatively, cook in the broiler.

In a small cooking pan, fry the onions and garlic in the remaining oil until they start to brown. Add the tomatoes and cook on low heat for 5 to 10 minutes, or until they soften into a sauce. Season with salt and pepper.

Combine the browned chicken pieces with coconut milk in a large pan and simmer for 5 to 10 minutes. Add the onion and tomato sauce to the chicken and coconut. Stir well, decrease the heat, and simmer slowly for 30 to 40 minutes, or until the coconut sauce reduces and the chicken becomes tender.

Pour the stew into a serving dish, and top with fresh cilantro. Serve hot.

The Struggle for Kenya

Coastal Kenya was settled as early as the seventh century A.D. by Persian and Arab traders on their endless quest for ivory and slaves. The first Europeans to arrive were the Portuguese in the sixteenth century. They constantly warred with the Arab population, and their position was further weakened by the growth of English naval power in the Indian Ocean. The Portuguese were finally driven out of Kenya in the seventeenth century. The coastal area came under control of the sultan of Oman, and a flourishing trade in ivory and slaves was soon established.

East Africa is completely different from the arid wilderness, deserts, or humid tropical forests of northern, central, and western Africa. The region enjoys a tropical climate that is dry and sunny. It favors the growth of exotic trees such as the African camphor, pencil cedar, baobab, and podo, which are found throughout the region.

TANZANIA

OFFICIAL TITLE: United Republic of Tanzania (a union of Tanganyika and the islands of Zanzibar, Pemba, and Mafia)

CAPITAL CITY: Dodoma (the former capital was Dar es Salaam)

OFFICIAL LANGUAGES: Kiswahili and English

CURRENCY: Tanzanian shilling (Tsh) = 100 cents

CASH CROPS FOR EXPORT: Tea, coffee, sugarcane, sisal, rubber, pyrethrum, cashew nuts, and spices and cloves from Zanzibar

FOOD CROPS: Corn, millet, sorghum, rice, cassava, peanuts, coconuts, yams, vegetables, plantains, bananas, livestock, poultry, and fresh fish

TOTAL LAND AREA: 364,094 square miles

Papaya Soup

Tanzanian food is not easy to describe: it may be best to classify it as a local variation on universal African food with a strong tropical slant. Because of the wide variety of fruits available in this country, recipes have been developed to use them. This unusual but delicious soup made from papaya is an example. It can be served hot or cold.

SERVES 4 TO 6

1 medium to large, firm, unripe papaya

1 teaspoon butter

3 shallots, minced

2 cups vegetable stock

Salt

Freshly ground black pepper

1 cup heavy cream

1 teaspoon chopped fresh chives

Peel the papaya, discard the seeds, and cut it into pieces. In a medium pan, heat the butter and fry the papaya and onion without browning. Add the stock, season with salt and pepper, and simmer until the papaya is soft. Put the mixture into a blender, and blend until smooth. Add $1/2$ cup of the cream and mix in.

If serving cold, let stand in a cool place until cold. Lightly pour on the remainder of the cream, and sprinkle the chopped chives on top before serving.

If serving hot, return to the stove and heat on low. When it is hot, add the rest of the cream, and garnish with the chives before serving.

The Spice Isle

Most of mainland Tanzania consists of a plateau of which the Great Rift Valley is a dominant feature. To the north near the border with Kenya is Mount Kilimanjaro, Africa's highest mountain, and on the border with Uganda, Lake Victoria, the largest lake in Africa. Several islands are offshore, including Zanzibar, the Spice Island, and Pemba. Zanzibar has lured travelers to its exotic shores for centuries. Under the Arabs in the mid-nineteenth century, the island became the most important trade center on the East African coast, supplying much of the world's cloves. It was also infamous for being the largest slaving entrepôt of Africa's eastern coast.

Cream of Banana Soup

MTORI

Pronounced m-tory, *this banana soup is a traditional dish from the Kilimanjaro region. It is very popular with nursing mothers, and while the men traditionally consider it feminine to take liquid foods, an exception is made for this soup because it is so delicious. Their excuse is that the men are helping their wives eat well!*

SERVES 4 TO 6

1 pound (500 g) lean beef, diced

2 large soup bones

6 cups cold water

1 tablespoon vegetable oil

5 green, unripe bananas or plantains

1 yellow onion, minced

1 large ripe tomato, blanched, peeled and minced

Salt

Freshly ground black pepper

1 teaspoon butter

Put the meat, bones, and water into a large pan and bring to a boil. Simmer for 1 1/2 hours to make a concentrated stock.

Rub the oil on your hands to prevent staining from the raw banana sap when you peel them. Peel and cut the bananas into thin strips. Strain the stock and remove the meat and bones. Discard the bones and save the meat.

In a large pan, combine the stock with the banana strips, onion, and tomato, and season with salt and pepper. Simmer on medium heat until all the ingredients are cooked and very soft.

Remove from the heat and whisk or blend together into a creamy soup. Add the reserved cooked meat. Taste and adjust the seasoning. Add the butter, stir through, and return to the heat. Reheat and serve hot.

Plantain and Coconut Beef Stew

Many African recipes are based on bananas or plantains. This one, n'dizi ya na nyama *(pronounced* ndee-zi yah nah n-yahmah*), is from the northern, western, and southern regions of Tanzania, where many bananas are grown. In Africa, plantains are an important crop and are preferred in cooking. You may substitute bananas, particularly unripe ones (ripe bananas are rarely used). Plantains are larger and thicker than bananas, and are not eaten raw.*

SERVES 4 TO 6

2 pounds (1 kg) lean beef, diced

1 cup cold water

Salt

Freshly ground black pepper

2 tablespoons vegetable oil

2 large yellow onions, minced

1 large tomato, blanched, peeled, and chopped

2 cups coconut milk

5 firm plantains or green, unripe bananas

1/2 cup peas

In a medium pan, combine the meat and the water, season with salt and pepper, and cook until tender. Set aside.

Heat the oil in a large pan and fry the onions without browning. Add the tomato and the meat mixture and adjust the seasoning to taste. Continue cooking until the tomato softens. Add the coconut milk, stirring continuously until the mixture boils.

Peel and cut the plantains into large pieces. Add the plantains and peas to the stew. Decrease the heat and simmer for 10 to 15 minutes, or until the plantains are cooked but not mushy.

Serve hot as a nutritious and filling stew.

Thick Corn Porridge

UGALI

Tanzania produces more corn (maize) than any other country in East Africa. Ugali *is a stiff, steamed porridge usually made from corn and is a staple of the diet, eaten by 90 percent of the population. Because* ugali *is inexpensive, poorer people can afford to combine it with* mchicha *(a variety of spinach) sauces and be sure of one good meal a day.* Ugali *can be served hot or, after it has cooled, it can be fried, giving it a different texture.*

Ugali is eaten all over East Africa and is known by different names in different regions: mealie-meal in southern Africa; sadza *in Zimbabwe; and* banku *in West Africa.* Ugali *may occasionally be made from* gari, *millet, or sorghum flour.*

SERVES 4

4 cups water or milk and water combined

4 tablespoons butter

Salt (optional)

3 cups cormeal, millet, *gari* (coarse cassava powder), or sorghum flour

Bring 3 cups of the water to a boil in a large, heavy-based pan with has a long handle for easier handling. Add the butter and season with salt.

Put 2 cups of the cornmeal into a bowl, and add the remaining water. Using a wooden spoon, stir to form a smooth, thick paste.When the water in the pan boils, pour in the thick paste and stir quickly and firmly for about 1 minute. Bring the mixture to a boil. Gradually add the remaining flour and mix, stirring continuously, until it thickens sufficiently to form a stiff dough. Caution: this stage requires a lot of wrist power and firm stirring.

The consistency can vary according to taste by adding more or less flour and/or more water. When cooked, the porridge should not stick to the sides of the pan.

Serve hot with meat stew and/or vegetables. Shape into balls with an ice-cream scoop, and serve surrounded by the meat and vegetables.

Spinach with Coconut

MCHICHA NA NAZI

Spinach is eaten widely all over Africa in a variety of forms: in combination with meat, fish, other vegetables, or on its own with seasonings. Michicha na nazi *(pronounced* m-chi-cha nah nahzi) *is a kind of spinach from the small island of Lamu off the coast of Kenya.*

SERVES 4

1 large bunch fresh spinach, or 1 pound frozen spinach, thawed

1 cup coconut milk

4 tablespoons ghee (Indian cooking butter) or butter

1 white onion, diced

1 tomato, diced

1 teaspoon curry powder

If you are using fresh spinach, remove the stalks and wash thoroughly. In a large pan, cook the fresh spinach in the coconut milk for about 5 minutes and drain well. Reserve the coconut milk.

In a medium pan, heat the ghee and fry the onion, tomato, and curry powder for about 5 minutes. Add the cooked spinach or the frozen spinach (thawed and drained) and the coconut milk. Stir all ingredients well and cook for 15 minutes over low heat.

Serve hot with rice and fried fish dishes.

The Legend of Mount Kilimanjaro

Mount Kilimanjaro has two peaks: one high and the other lower and with a serrated edge. Legend has it that many years ago, the peaks were sisters. Kibo was the name of the taller one, and Mawenzi was the smaller, although they were once the same height.

Mawenzi was very lazy and visited her sister every day on the pretext of borrowing some hot coals or firewood. Invariably, however, she managed to linger not only for lunch, but for dinner too. After several years of feeding her sister twice a day, Kibo had

enough. Grabbing a traditional flat wooden spoon, she hit Mawenzi several times on the head. To this day, Mawenzi is shorter than her sister and has notches on her head—a testament to her laziness.

African Spinach

Many Africans refer to the leaves of local root vegetables as "spinach," although these vegetables might be quite different from what Western cooks know as spinach or swiss chard.

The triangular leaves of the taro plant, known in the Ashanti language as *kontomire*, are called spinach in Ghana and other parts of

West Africa. In Egypt, the local plant *molohia* can be replaced with spinach. In Tanzania *mchicha,* a staple green leaf rather like spinach that grows prolifically, is also known locally as spinach.

The leaf of the taro plant is popular across the Atlantic too, in such countries as Trinidad. Known in Tanzania as *dasheen*, it is one of the

varieties of plants that are generically called spinach.

Spinach is used in many recipes throughout Africa and wherever African cooking has spread. Don't worry if you are unable to find the local variety of plant, because although the taste and texture may not be exactly the same, spinach will do just as well.

Pumpkin Leaves and Flowers in Cream

MBOGA YA MABOGA

Tanzanians are quite flexible in their use of ingredients, probably because of the influence of other cuisines. Not only do they frequently combine foods in ways unusual to the rest of the continent, but they use, for example, parts of plants that are not valued elsewhere—hence this delicacy (pronounced mboh-gah ya ma-boh-gah*) based on the pumpkin plant from central and southern Tanzania. This dish is often served as an accompaniment to ugali* (page 113) *and stew.*

SERVES 4

1 pound pumpkin leaves

8 pumpkin flowers, cleaned

1 tablespoon vegetable oil

1 large yellow onion, chopped

1 teaspoon ground turmeric

1 fresh red chile (optional)

1 large tomato, blanched, peeled, and chopped

Salt

1/4 cup heavy cream

Wash the pumpkin leaves and flowers and remove fibrous and spiky parts and stalks. Finely shred the leaves. In a large pan, blanch the leaves in boiling salted water to cover for 5 minutes, then drain well and set aside.

Heat the oil in a medium pan and fry the onion until translucent, but not brown. Add the turmeric, chile, and tomato, and season with salt. Decrease the heat and simmer on low, stirring frequently, until the tomato is cooked, about 10 minutes.

Add the pumpkin leaves and the cream, and continue cooking on low heat for about 10 minutes. Stir in the pumpkin flowers and cook for 5 minutes.

Remove from the heat and let stand, covered, for 3 to 4 minutes. Remove the flowers from the stew and arrange them decoratively on top.

Serve hot.

Plantain Chips

These chips are a favorite of young and old alike. In Africa, more plantain chips are eaten than potato chips! These are a fantastic accompaniment to predinner drinks.

SERVES 4 TO 6

2 semiripe plantains or
   bananas

Salt

Freshly ground black pepper

Vegetable oil, for deep-frying

Peel the plantains or bananas and cut into very thin rings. Season with salt and pepper. Fry in very hot vegetable oil until crisp (not necessarily golden). Remove from the heat and drain on paper towels.

Serve hot or cold.

Banana Fritters

Around the world, banana fritters vary in preparation styles, but this mashed variety (pronounced cha-pah-ti yah ndee-zi tahmu) *is different and fairly common in Africa.*

SERVES 4

3 large, very ripe bananas

¼ cup milk

⅔ cup superfine sugar

4 or 5 tablespoons cornstarch

1 teaspoon freshly grated nutmeg

Vegetable oil, for frying

Peel the bananas, cut into halves, put in a mixing bowl, and mash into a thick, coarse paste with your fingers or a wooden spoon (or an electric blender).

Stir in the milk, sugar, 2 tablespoons cornstarch, and the nutmeg and mix together thoroughly. You may need to add more cornstarch; the finished mixture should be thick and slightly coarse (which is why it is preferable to mash the bananas initially with your fingers).

Heat a shallow layer of vegetable oil in a skillet until the oil ripples, but does not smoke. Fry 1 tablespoon of the fritter mixture as a test. If it burns immediately, the oil is too hot, so decrease the heat. If it does not burn immediately but browns nicely, turn it over and cook the other side until both sides are golden and the fritter is firm.

Continue to fry the remaining mixture in small batches. Drain the fritters on paper napkins or on a wire rack, and keep them in a warm oven until all fritters have been cooked. Serve hot.

Savory Pumpkin–Sweet Potato Fritters

This is a light snack to stave off hunger. It's an excellent after-school snack for children, and also works well as an appetizer. By combining a very sweet pumpkin with purple-skinned sweet potatoes, the fritters will be quite sweet.

SERVES 4

1 cup mashed cooked pumpkin or sweet potato, or a combination

2 eggs

1 cup flour

1 teaspoon baking powder

Salt

Freshly ground black pepper

Vegetable oil, for frying

Mix together the mashed pumpkin, eggs, flour, baking powder and a healthy pinch of salt and pepper to form a thick paste.

Heat a shallow layer of vegetable oil in a large, heavy-based skillet until it is hot and starts to ripple. Or heat a skillet until it is very hot and spray the inside of the hot pan with oil.

Fry spoonfuls of the mixture about 3 minutes, or until crisp and brown. Turn during cooking so the fritters brown evenly on both sides.

Remove the cooked fritters and drain on paper towels. Serve hot alone or to accompany another dish.

Coconut Fish Curry

This curry (pronounced sah-ma-kih wah nahzi*) is popular among the coastal dwellers of Tanzania and on Zanzibar, the "Island of Spices." With its location on the eastern coast of the African continent, Tanzania has been influenced by the cultures and cuisines of many other trading and seagoing nations, including India, Portugal, and Persia (Iran), so not all the local recipes are strictly Tanzanian in origin. The result is a cuisine that is varied and exotic.*

SERVES 4

2 pounds (1 kg) firm, white-fleshed fish

Salt

3 tablespoons vegetable oil

1 white onion, chopped

2 cloves garlic, crushed

1 tablespoon curry powder

2 tablespoons tomato paste

1 or 2 fresh red chiles (optional)

Juice of ½ lemon

2 cups coconut milk

Clean and rinse the fish, then season it with salt. Heat the oil in a medium pan and brown the fish. Set it aside and keep warm. In the same oil, fry the onion until brown.

Add the garlic and stir; cook for 1 minute, then add the curry powder, tomato paste, chiles, and lemon juice. Mix well and continue stirring to prevent the mixture from burning. Cook for 2 to 3 minutes.

Add the coconut milk and stir until it boils. Decrease the heat and add the fried fish. Simmer for about 10 minutes, or until the flavors concentrate and the sauce thickens to a creamy consistency. Serve hot.

Chicken Curry

This dish is a family favorite. Just about all my friends who have eaten it at my home have requested the recipe to take home! This curry is delicious served with steaming-hot jasmine rice.

SERVES 4 TO 6

8 chicken wings each divided
    in half, tips discarded

2 cups cold water

CHICKEN SEASONING

1 1/2 tablespoons sweet paprika

1 1/2 tablespoons curry powder

1 tablespoon ground coriander

1 teaspoon chile powder or
    cayenne pepper

3 large cloves garlic, minced

1 red onion, minced

2 teaspoons salt

1 teaspoon freshly ground
    black pepper

Juice of 1 lime

CURRY SAUCE

3/4 cup vegetable oil

3 large red onions, minced

2 cloves garlic, minced

3 green chiles, seeded and
    minced

1 fresh red chile, minced

1 tablespoon curry powder

1 1/2 cups ripe red tomatoes,
    blanched, peeled, and
    chopped

1/2 cup coconut milk

6 curry leaves

6 to 8 green cardamom pods

Juice of 1 lime

ACCOMPANIMENTS

6 cups hot cooked jasmine or
    basmati rice

1 cucumber, peeled and finely
    diced

2 cups plain yogurt

1/2 cup mango or lime pickle

1/2 cup sweet mango chutney

2 fresh tomatoes, diced

1/2 cup toasted shredded
    coconut

1 mango, peeled and diced

1/2 cup chopped fresh mint

1 fresh lime, cut into 6 wedges

Fresh green salad of choice

Put the chicken pieces in a large bowl, and add all the ingredients of the chicken seasoning. Using clean hands, mix the seasoning and chicken pieces thoroughly. Cover and set aside to marinate in a refrigerator overnight; if you are pressed for time, marinate for 1 to 2 hours.

Transfer the marinated chicken to a medium-large pan. Add the water and bring to a boil. Decrease the heat and simmer gently on low.

Meanwhile, to make the curry sauce, heat the oil in a large skillet and fry the onions, garlic, and red and green chiles until soft and browning. Stir in the curry powder and cook for 1 to 2 minutes before adding the tomatoes, coconut milk, curry leaves, and cardamom pods. Simmer for about 5 minutes.

Add the sauce and the lime juice to the chicken, and continue simmering on medium to low heat for 30 to 40 minutes, or until the sauce reduces and thickens and the chicken is well cooked and soft.

Serve hot with the rice and any combination of the other listed accompaniments.

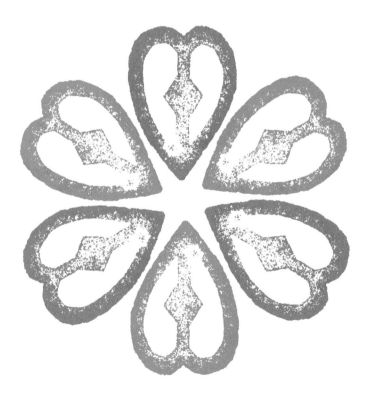

Zanzibari Chicken

The spice island, Zanzibar, boasts a delicious, eclectic cuisine that is aromatically laced with a never-ending supply of spices grown on the island. The cuisine is a rich mixture of Arab, African, and Indian, a testament to the fascinating history of this island off the Tanzanian coast. I like to eat this chicken dish with Savory Pumpkin–Sweet Potato Fritters (page 119) and a green salad.

SERVES 4

5 to 6 lemons

8 chicken pieces (such as drumsticks, thighs, and wings)

Vegetable oil, for deep-frying

Flour, for dredging

CHICKEN SEASONING

3 cloves garlic, minced

3 or 4 hot chiles, seeded and minced

2-inch long piece fresh ginger, peeled and very finely grated

1-inch long piece fresh turmeric root, peeled and minced

Juice and finely grated zest of 1 lime

2 lime leaves

Sea salt

4 cups cold water

BATTER

4 fresh eggs

$1/2$ teaspoon ground cloves

$1/2$ teaspoon ground cinnamon

$1/2$ teaspoon freshly grated nutmeg

$1/2$ teaspoon salt

Cut the lemons into quarters and use them to rub the chicken pieces thoroughly to clean them.

In a large, heavy-based pan, combine all the ingredients for the chicken seasoning with the chicken pieces and bring to a boil. Decrease the heat and simmer, uncovered, until the chicken pieces are cooked but still firm (not disintegrated) and most of the liquid is gone. Remove from the heat and let cool.

Preheat the oven to 300°F/160°C.

To make the batter, lightly whisk together the eggs, cloves, cinnamon, nutmeg, and salt. Heat some vegetable oil in a large skillet for deep-frying. It is ready when the oil is very hot and the surface is rippling. Coat each chicken piece lightly with flour. Shake off excess flour, dip the chicken pieces into the batter mix, and carefully lower small batches into the hot oil. Fry, taking care to turn each piece until golden brown and crisp.

Remove from the oil and drain on paper towels. Arrange in an ovenproof dish, and keep warm in the preheated oven until all the chicken pieces are done.

Serve hot.

Beef and Spinach

Mchicha *is a staple green, rather like spinach, that is eaten by everyone in Tanzania because it is cheap and easy to grow. Indeed, the more you harvest the small shoots, the more prolifically the plant grows. One can find the plant everywhere, including backyards, and it can be used in soups, casseroles, salads, pies, and with* ugali, *as well as in this beef and spinach dish (pronounced* m-chi-cha nah nyah-mah*). If* mchicha *is unavailable, spinach is a successful substitute.*

SERVES 4

3 tablespoons vegetable oil

1 large yellow or white onion, minced

1 pound (500 g) lean steak, cut into 2-inch strips

1 teaspoon peeled and grated fresh ginger

Salt

Freshly ground black pepper

2 ripe tomatoes, blanched, peeled, and minced

1 green bell pepper, seeded and minced

1 large bunch *mchicha* or spinach, stalks removed and chopped

Thick Corn Porridge (page 113), as accompaniment

In a medium pan, heat the oil over medium heat and fry the onion without browning. Add the meat and ginger and season with salt and pepper. Fry until the meat browns. Add the tomatoes and bell pepper and continue frying until the tomatoes are cooked and the meat is tender, 25 to 30 minutes. Add the *mchicha* and mix well.

Serve immediately with the porridge.

Beef and Plantains

MACHALARI

This is a favorite of the Chagga people who live around the base of Mount Kilimanjaro in Tanzania. It is fairly basic, but very tasty. The Chagga grow a variety of bananas, including plantains or vegetable bananas, and each type has its specific use. For this recipe, which was shown to me when I was in Tanzania, the locals used mshare *and* mnyanyele.

SERVES 4

1 pound (500 g) lean red meat, diced into 1-inch cubes

Salt

1 teaspoon freshly ground black pepper

4 cups meat stock

2 yellow or white onions, peeled and finely diced

2 large, green plantains, peeled and cut into 4-inch cubes

4 tomatoes, blanched, peeled, and puréed

1 cup coconut milk

Salad greens, for garnish

Fresh chile peppers, for garnish

Season the meat with salt and pepper. Place the meat in a Dutch oven or deep pan over low to medium heat, and dry cook for about 3 minutes to seal the meat. Add the stock and half the onions, cover partially, and boil until the meat is cooked and tender, but not too soft. During cooking, add small amounts of water or stock as needed to keep the meat from drying out.

When the meat is cooked, add the remaining onions, plantain cubes, tomatoes, and coconut milk. Continue to cook until the plantain is also cooked and tender and most of the liquid has reduced into a creamy sauce. Taste and adjust the seasoning before serving.

Serve hot, garnished with greens and peppers of your choice.

Chilled Banana Cream

With so many Tanzanian recipes based on bananas or plantains, you could almost make an entire meal from these fruits! Cream of Banana Soup (page 111) and Plantain and Coconut Beef Stew (page 112) could be followed by this dessert. Essentially, this is a vanilla-egg custard that is mixed with whipped cream, sugar, mashed bananas, and flavoring and then frozen.

In the highlands and areas of Africa without refrigerators, desserts are covered and put outside in the cold night air. At daybreak they are gathered, covered with cloth, and kept in a cool, dark part of the house until serving time.

SERVES 4

EGG CUSTARD

1 cup milk

2 eggs

2 tablespoons superfine sugar

2 or 3 drops vanilla extract

BANANA CREAM

Egg custard

2 very ripe bananas, peeled and thoroughly mashed

1 tablespoon superfine sugar (optional)

1 cup heavy cream

3 or 4 drops food coloring of choice (optional)

Bananas, peeled and decoratively cut, as accompaniment

To make the egg custard, heat the milk in a small pan almost to the boiling point, but do not let it boil. Break the eggs into the hot milk, add the sugar and vanilla extract, and blend or whisk to a creamy mixture. Simmer slowly on very low heat, stirring continuously, until it thickens into a smooth custard. Remove from the heat.

To make the banana cream, thoroughly mix together the egg custard, mashed bananas, and sugar. Blend in the whipped cream and the food coloring. Transfer into a serving dish and freeze.

Decorate and serve with the bananas.

Plantain Wine

Yes, you can make a wine from plantains and bananas! This particular version is made with plantains and literally means "alcohol with bananas." The recipe is pronounced pom-bay yah ndee-zi. *It is delicious and can be drunk after three months. I prefer to let the process take longer—up to six months—to allow the wine to mature and develop a stronger flavor.*

MAKES 24 TO 28
GLASSES

7 very ripe plantains or bananas, peeled and finely sliced

5 quarts cold water

4 pounds sugar

4 1-inch-wide strips soft toast

1 tablespoon fresh yeast

In a very large pot, boil the plantains in the water for 20 minutes. Strain and add the sugar to the liquid. Set aside to cool. Spread both sides of each strip of toast with yeast and drop them into the strained liquid.

Lightly cover the jar with a piece of cheesecloth and store in a cool, safe place for 1 week. Strain the liquid after 1 week, and store in an airtight container for 3 weeks. Open and strain for the third time. Store in an airtight container for an additional month.

Finally, open and strain for the fourth and last time, then bottle as wine and cork. You may now chill the wine and serve it as normal; however, the longer it is left, the more mature it will become, so serve it when it suits you. Personally, I prefer the total process to take 3 to 6 months.

ZIMBABWE

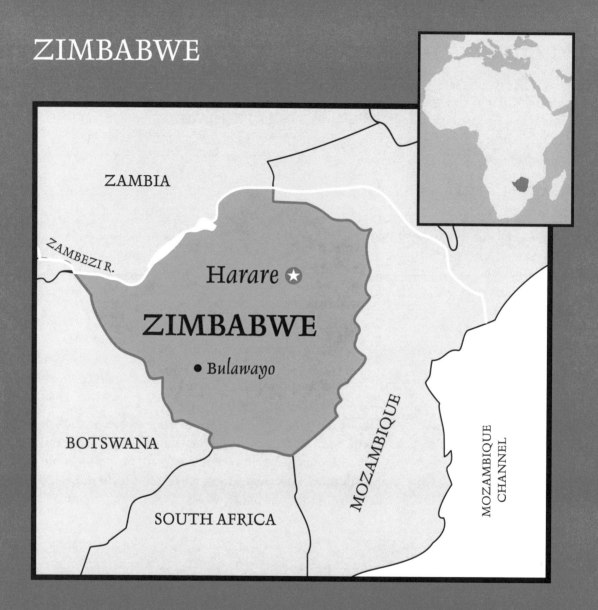

OFFICIAL TITLE: Republic of Zimbabwe

CAPITAL CITY: Harare (the name of a former African ruler of the area, it means "one who does not sleep")

OFFICIAL LANGUAGE: English, although Shona and Ndebele are widely spoken

CURRENCY: Zimbabwe dollar (Z$) = 100 cents

CASH CROPS FOR EXPORT: Corn, wheat, coffee, cotton, soybeans, peanuts, and tobacco

FOOD CROPS: Corn, wheat, soybeans, peanuts, cattle, and fish farming

TOTAL LAND AREA: 150,966 square miles

Chicken and Peanut-Vegetable Stew

HUKU NE DOVI

Zimbabwe is a landlocked nation, so there is a greater emphasis on meat in the local cuisine in contrast to other countries that have abundant supplies of ocean fish. This dish (pronounced whoo-ku nay dorvi*) is more frequently eaten for dinner than for lunch by the Shonas of Zimbabwe, and it is always accompanied by a carbohydrate dish such as rice or Sadza Dumplings (page 135), a popular kind of dumpling made from millet flour.*

In this part of the world, chicken is generally considered a delicacy, and when it is served slightly tough, it confirms that your hosts have served you an authentic free-range chicken and not a processed one!

SERVES 8

1 chicken, 3¹/₃-pounds (1.5 kg)

Salt

¹/₂ cup vegetable oil

2 yellow onions, diced

2 tomatoes, blanched, peeled, and diced

¹/₂ pound mushrooms, cleaned

Dried vegetables (optional) (opposite)

1¹/₂ cups cold water

³/₄ cup peanut paste or peanut butter

Boiling water, as needed

1 fresh red chile (optional)

Rinse the chicken and cut into 8 serving pieces. Season with salt. In a large pan, heat the oil and fry the chicken pieces and onions, turning the chicken until evenly browned. Stir in the tomatoes and cook for about 3 minutes. Add the whole mushrooms and the dried vegetables. Stir well for 1 minute. Add the water and simmer slowly for approximately 30 minutes, or until the chicken is very tender and nearly cooked.

Put the peanut butter into a bowl with enough boiling water to blend it into a smooth, runny paste. Add this paste and the chile when the chicken is tender and almost cooked. Mix well and simmer on low heat, stirring regularly to prevent lumps and burning. Cook for about 20 minutes, or until the sauce has thickened and the chicken is cooked.

Serve hot.

The House of Stone

The name Zimbabwe means "house of stone." Lying between the Limpopo and Zambezi Rivers in the southern heart of Africa, Zimbabwe is more fortunate than many other African countries because it is self-sufficient in food.

Zimbabwe is the home of great stone ruins built more than eight centuries ago by the Shona people, descendants of a culture that flourished during the Iron Age. The Shona still form the dominant racial group in the country, followed in number by the Ndebele.

Wonders of Zimbabwe include the Chinhoi Caves and the massive Victoria Falls, known as *mosi oa tunya*, or "the smoke that thunders."

Winter Vegetables

Although Zimbabwe is fortunate in its capacity to be self-sufficient in food, its agriculture is still dependent on the seasonal variation in rainfall; the winter dry season can lead to crippling drought. One method of dealing with this period of little growth is to dry various foods harvested after the rainy season.

In Zimbabwe, as in other countries, vegetables harvested during summer and autumn are dried for later use in winter.

Some of these vegetables are:

Bowara: These pumpkin leaves, excluding the *nhopi* variety, are very soft and are frequently mixed with beef in stews, combined with the flesh of baby pumpkins and pumpkin flowers, or served with chicken.

Derere: This is the Zimbabwean name for okra.

Kovo: A large-leafed vegetable the size of a cabbage, but bigger, sweeter, and lighter in texture and taste.

Nyovhi: This wild plant is indigenous to Zimbabwe and has small, narrow, green leaves. It is important to harvest the leaves at the right season or they will taste bitter. Early *nyovhi* shoots usually herald the arrival of summer and the rainy season. *Nyovhi* is frequently eaten cooked and mixed with mushrooms and baby pumpkins or in goat stew.

Steak and Bean Stew

NYAMA NE NYEMBA

There are innumerable varieties of beans, and they are an ever-present favorite of many soul food menus. Beans are favored for their protein and fiber content, and are easy to grow. Since many varieties are drought-resistant, they are a staple of the African diet. Beans are versatile, delicious, and can be cooked dried or fresh in a wide range of dishes. This stew is a Zimbabwean specialty.

SERVES 4 TO 6

3 yellow or white onions, thinly sliced

3 tablespoons vegetable oil

2 pounds (1 kg) beef shoulder or pork spareribs, diced

2 cloves garlic, crushed

1 fresh green chile, crushed

3 tablespoons curry powder

2 tomatoes, sliced or diced

Salt

Freshly ground black pepper

2 pounds (1 kg) dried kidney beans, cooked

Juice of 1 lemon

6 cups hot boiled long-grain rice, as accompaniment

Sadza Dumplings (page 135), as accompaniment

In a stew pot, brown the onions in the oil until golden brown. Add the meat and sauté over medium heat for about 5 minutes, stirring continuously. Decrease the heat and cook gently for 15 to 20 minutes. Add the garlic, chile, and curry powder and cook for about 3 minutes. Stir in the tomatoes and cook for another 3 minutes.

Season with salt and pepper, stir in the cooked beans, and simmer over low heat for about 15 minutes.

Transfer to a serving dish and drizzle the lemon juice all over the top.

Garnish as you wish and serve with boiled rice or the dumplings, or alone as a nutritious meal.

Spicy Meat and Vegetable Stew

MAHOBHO OR SADZA NDIURAYE

Mahobho *means "plenty," while this dish's alternative name,* sadza ndiuraye *(because the dish is always served with* sadza *dumplings), translates as "sadza don't kill me!" A Zimbabwean friend of mine, Gus, swears this recipe makes a wonderful hangover cure. I suppose this could be where the name "sadza don't kill me" comes from: the dish is designed to kill or cure you quickly—whichever way, it will put you out of your misery!*

SERVES 4 TO 6

SAUCE

2 tablespoons vegetable oil

1/2 head cabbage, thinly sliced

1 turnip, peeled and diced

1 large white onion, diced

2 fresh green chiles,
    thinly sliced

2 large tomatoes, blanched,
    peeled, and diced

1 tablespoon honey

1 3/4 cups hot water

Salt

Freshly ground black pepper

MEAT

2 tablespoons vegetable oil

3 1/3 pounds (1.5 kg) lean
    stewing steak, diced

1 large yellow onion, diced

2 potatoes, peeled and
    coarsely chopped

Sadza Dumplings (page 135),
    as accompaniment

To make the sauce, heat the oil in a large pan. Lightly fry the cabbage, turnip, onion, and green chiles for 3 to 4 minutes. Stir in the tomatoes and cook until they are soft. Mix the honey and hot water together and add to the vegetables. Season with salt and pepper. Simmer for approximately 10 minutes, or until the vegetables are soft and cooked (cook for less time if you prefer crunchier vegetables). Set aside.

To cook the meat, heat the oil in a pan over medium heat, and sauté the steak and the onion for 5 minutes. Add the potatoes and stir for 5 minutes. Add the prepared sauce. Cook over low heat, stirring occasionally, for about 10 minutes, or until meat and vegetables are cooked and tender. Serve hot with the dumplings.

Pumpkin-Peanut Sauce

NHOPI DOVI

A mashamba *is a Zimbabwean variety of pumpkin that bears an uncanny resemblance to a melon and has green flesh.* Nhopi dovi *is a Shona recipe; the Ndebele people have a similar recipe, which uses a different pumpkin called* mbaqanga. *It has yellow flesh and creates a much thicker dish. Both recipes are very popular with children.*

SERVES 4

4 cups peeled and diced *mashamba* or butternut squash

2 cups cold water

2 cups peanut paste or peanut butter

Salt or sugar

In a medium pan, boil the *mashamba* in the water until cooked thoroughly, very soft, and ready to mash. Drain away the excess water. Stir in the peanut paste. Thoroughly mash both to form a creamy, smooth paste. Depending on your taste, season with salt or sugar to make it savory or sweet.

Serve hot or cold as a lunch. When cold, it sets to a jellylike mass.

The Legend of the Fig Tree

A man of Zimbabwe searched every day for food for his family. As food was so scarce, he preferred to sleep under a tree during his midday break. One day his hunger woke him. In desperation he sang, "somebody feed me; please feed me before I die." A miracle occurred! The fig tree suddenly grew fruit that dropped around him. With joy, he ate his fill, but selfishly did not take home any fruit for his family. That evening he was too full to eat his meal.

He told no one about the miracle tree but returned every day to sing to it and gorge on fruit. And every day he returned home too full to eat with his family. Seeing that he remained healthy, his children grew suspicious and secretly followed him. They saw what happened and decided to teach their father a lesson. The next day before he arrived, the children sang to the tree and gathered the fruit as it fell. Then they climbed the tree to wait.

When their father arrived, he sang to the tree, but instead of fruit he was pelted with stones. That night he ate his *sadza* in silence!

Sadza Dumplings

Due to its enormous popularity, sadza *is regarded as Zimbabwe's national dish. Like the West African* banku, *the East African* ugali, *the Zambian* ntsima, *and the South African* mealie-meal, sadza *is a stiff, steamed dumpling made from white corn flour or* rapoko *and served with stews or roasted meats, fish, or vegetables and sauce.*

SERVES 4

10 cups cold water

6 cups white corn flour, *rapoko* (red millet flour), or millet flour

Bring 6 cups of the water to a boil in a large, heavy-based pan with a long handle for easy handling. Mix 3 cups of the corn flour with the remaining water to form a smooth paste. Add this paste to the boiling water, stirring vigorously to avoid lumps, until it boils again. Cover and continue to boil for 5 minutes.

Gradually add the remaining corn flour, one-quarter at a time, stirring thoroughly and firmly until the whole mixture thickens. You need a firm wrist; as the mixture thickens, the porridge gets firmer and more difficult to stir. Decrease the heat, cover the pan, and cook for another 3 minutes.

Wet a small bowl with cold water and use it to form the mixture into individual portions. Alternatively, you can serve the *sadza* as one large family portion. Serve hot.

Zimbabwean Saying

Hunge rakatsigir wa nemuto:
"For sadza to enter, it must be supported by the sauce—always!"

Peri-Peri Chicken

Peri-peri *sauce is a very popular spicy seasoning in southern Africa, particularly Portuguese southern Africa. It is most often used to season chicken pieces or whole birds, but you can also use it to season just about anything. For a milder marinade, use less cayenne and more sweet paprika.*

SERVES 4 TO 6

PERI-PERI SAUCE

4 tablespoons freshly squeezed lemon juice

4 tablespoons olive or vegetable oil

1 tablespoon cayenne pepper

1 tablespoon sweet paprika

1 heaped teaspoon sea salt

1 teaspoon freshly ground black pepper

1 teaspoon garlic powder

2 pounds (1 kg) chicken pieces (such as thigh, wings, or breasts), or 1 whole chicken, 3 pounds (1.5 kg)

Combine all the ingredients except the chicken in a small mixing bowl, and mix to form a paste. This is the peri-peri sauce.

If using chicken pieces, pour the sauce over the chicken pieces and toss so each piece is well coated. Cover and set aside to marinate for a few hours in the refrigerator, preferably overnight. Bake, barbecue, grill, fry, or cook according to personal preference.

For a whole chicken, spread the *peri-peri* sauce between the skin and the meat first, then coat the outside of the chicken with the remaining sauce. Cover and let marinate in a refrigerator for at least 30 minutes to 1 hour or longer before cooking. The longer you marinate the meat, the tastier it is when cooked!

Preheat the oven to 400°F/200°C.

Place the chicken in a large roasting pan. Roast in the oven for 35 to 45 minutes, or until the thigh releases clear juices when pricked, and an instant-read thermometer reads 170° to 175°F/105° to 110°C when inserted into the thigh. Remove from the oven, let stand for 10 minutes, and then carve.

Serve hot.

NOTE: You can, of course, use *peri-peri* sauce as seasoning for vegetables, fish, or meat, or you can mix small portions of it with regular salad dressing to give a piquancy to a plain salad.

South African Cape Malay Meat Loaf

BOBOTIE

This much loved classic South African dish, pronounced berbouti *or* berbwerti, *has its origins in the Malay culture of Southeast Asia. The Dutch who founded the Cape in the mid-seventeenth century imported Malays as laborers, and, naturally, the Malays brought along many tasty recipes. Bobotie is one such recipe and is now firmly entrenched in South Africa's Cape Malay culinary repertoire. There are many variations, with ingredients varying from rolled oats versus bread and apples versus raisins to brown sugar versus white sugar. No matter—as simple as the recipe is, the end result is always delicious!*

SERVES 4 TO 6

1 cup rolled oats

1 cup milk

2 tablespoons vegetable oil or butter

1 large red onion, minced

1 tablespoon ground turmeric or mild curry powder

3 tablespoons brown sugar

2 sweet apples, peeled, cored, and minced

4 tablespoons raisins or pitted, chopped dates

1 1/2 pounds (750 g) lean ground beef

1 tablespoon water mixed with 1 tablespoon malt vinegar

Salt

Freshly ground black pepper

2 eggs

2 tablespoons slivered almonds

A few lemon or bay leaves, for garnish

Crisp, fresh green salad, as accompaniment

Preheat the oven to 350°F/180°C.

Soak the oats in the milk for about 15 minutes. Strain through a fine-mesh sieve and, using a wooden spoon, gently press down on the oats in the sieve to squeeze out excess milk. Reserve both the oats and milk. Cover and set aside.

In a large nonstick pan, heat the oil, add the onion, and fry on medium heat, stirring regularly, for 8 to 10 minutes, or until the onion softens. Stir in the turmeric first, followed by the sugar, apples, raisins, and the reserved oats.

Continue frying and stirring for 2 to 3 more minutes, then add the meat and the vinegar mixture. Stir well to mix all the ingredients thoroughly. Cook for about 5 minutes, taste, and season with salt and pepper.

Lightly grease an 8-inch baking dish, pour the mixture into it, and smooth the surface to make it even and neat.

Whisk together the reserved milk and the eggs. Lightly season with salt and pepper, and pour evenly over the surface of the meat mixture. Sprinkle with the almond slivers.

Bake in the preheated oven for approximately 45 minutes, or until well cooked. This meat loaf should be dry on the outside, but soft and moist inside. Remove from the oven. Garnish with lemon or bay leaves, and serve hot accompanied by the salad.

NIGERIA

OFFICIAL TITLE: Federal Republic of Nigeria

CAPITAL CITY: Abuja (new federal capital); Lagos is former capital/main port

OFFICIAL LANGUAGE: English, although Hausa, Yoruba, and Ibo are widely spoken

CURRENCY: Naira (N) = 100 kobo

CASH CROPS FOR EXPORT: Cocoa, coffee, cotton, rubber, palm oil, palm kernel, livestock, and poultry

FOOD CROPS: Sorghum, corn, rice, millet, wheat, yams, and peanuts

TOTAL LAND AREA: 356,758 square miles

Okra Soup

This dish is native to Nigeria and is based on meat, smoked fish, seafood, and vegetables, including, of course, okra. I'm convinced that along with the Ghanaian Okra Stew (page 12), it forms the basis of the now world-famous "gumbo" of New Orleans and the Caribbean. I recommend serving this soup with with Cornmeal Dumplings (page 21), Semolina Dumplings (page 22), or rice.

SERVES 6

1 pound (500 g) lean bone-in top round beef (see Note)

1/4 cup vegetable oil

3 yellow onions, minced

3 large ripe tomatoes, blanched, peeled, and puréed

1 pound okra, topped, tailed, and sliced into thin rounds

2 fresh red chiles, minced, or 2 tablespoons chile powder

1/2 ounce (15 g) salted beef

2 teaspoons tomato paste

4 cups cold water

Small piece of *kaawé* or local meat tenderizing stone (optional)

1 tablespoon ground dried shrimp

6 large fresh shrimp, peeled and deveined

1/4 pound (125 g) crayfish meat

1 to 2 pounds (500 g to 1 kg) smoked fish

Salt

Remove any fat and sinew from the meat, and cut into 2 1/2– 3-inch chunks. Leave the meat on the bone. Put the meat in a large pan and add the oil, and one-fourth each of the onions, tomatoes, okra, and chiles, and the salted beef. Sauté for about 10 minutes, stirring all the time, until the meat is browned on all sides.

In a blender, blend the remaining onions, tomatoes, chiles, and the tomato paste with the water, and add it to the meat mix with the *kaawé*. Bring to a boil, decrease the heat, and simmer for about 10 minutes. Add the rest of the okra and simmer for 20 minutes. Check to see if the meat is tender.

Add the dried shrimp, the fresh shrimp, the crayfish meat, and the smoked fish and continue to simmer for 10 to 15 minutes. Season with salt and continue simmering on low heat until the volume of water is reduced. You may need to add more water to help the meat cook until tender, depending on the type of meat. When all the ingredients are cooked, the soup should be creamy and chunky, with the flavors of okra, crayfish, and meat vying for attention.

Serve hot.

NOTE: You can also use lamb chops, lamb cutlets, skirt beef, or cubes of salted beef. Four pieces of salted, boiled pig's feet make the dish taste delicious.

The African Lifeline

Nigeria took its name from the Niger River, which is an important lifeline not only to Nigeria but also to the other African countries through which it flows: Sierra Leone, where the river rises, Guinea, Mali, and Niger.

Like many coastal West African countries, Nigeria suffered under the slave trade of the seventeenth and eighteenth centuries when the Portuguese, British, and other European nations established slave-trading stations in the rich delta of the Niger. These coastal stations served as collection points and embarkation stations for slave ships journeying across the Atlantic to the Americas and West Indies.

Such a variety of people and cultures make up Nigeria's population of ninety million that it is impossible to pick a national dish. Each area has its own regional favorite depending on tradition, custom, religion, and food availability. Available food varies according to the season: the "hungry season" occurs before the rains arrive in March to May, while the "season of surplus" follows the harvest in October and November.

The northern (and mostly Muslim) peoples' diets are based on beans, sorghum, and brown rice; the eastern, largely Ibo-speaking people eat *gari* (coarse cassava powder) dumplings and yams; the people in the southeast mostly prefer a seafood and yam stew; while the mainly Yoruba people in the southwest eat *gari* with local varieties of spinach and okra in stews or soups.

Urban dwellers tend to buy their food on the streets from "chop bars," street stalls, vendors, or in restaurants. The most popular foods are dishes based on cassava, yams, okra, beans, plantains, or skewered meat dishes.

Nigerian Beef Stew

It is very hard to pass up this rich Yoruba stew. (The Yoruba is one of the major traditional groups of southwestern Nigeria.) In West Africa, the word "stew" is so entrenched in the culinary vocabulary that many natives no longer use or remember the traditional words for certain dishes. Nowadays, a stew is any dish that is not a soup—be it a fish, chicken, beef, or vegetable dish—and which uses a red sauce with onion, tomato, and chile. Traditionally, this dish is served with boiled long-grain white rice.

SERVES 4

1 pound (500 g) good-quality lean beef, cut into large chunks

2 to 4 teaspoons chile powder

4 tablespoons cornstarch

Salt

3/4 cup vegetable oil

4 green onions, cut into narrow strips

4 large tomatoes, blanched, peeled, and puréed

2 cups cold water

4 teaspoons tomato paste

Season the meat with 2 teaspoons of the chile powder, 2 tablespoons of the cornstarch and salt. Heat the oil in a large heavy-based pan and sauté the meat until browned. Transfer the meat to a large bowl. Pour off the oil and reserve. Do not wash the pan. Add just enough water to cover the base of the pan and bring it to a boil over low heat. The boiling water will blend with the meat juices from the base of the pan. Transfer this juice to the fried meat.

Clean the pan and pour in the oil used to fry the meat. Blend in the rest of the cornstarch and gently heat. When the flour starts to brown, add the onions and sauté until browned. Quickly stir in the puréed tomatoes. Mix the water with the tomato paste and stir into the onions and tomatoes. Transfer the meat and juices to the pan and stir well. Taste the stew and season with salt and the remaining chile powder to taste. Simmer slowly for 10 minutes, or until meat is tender and the sauce has thickened.

Skim off any excess oil before serving. Serve hot.

Whitebait and Pepper Sauce

Like many West Africans, Nigerians are big eaters of fish. Whitebait is a favorite, and is referred to by the Ibo (native people) as Nwokelanya, *which means "little sparkly eye." When dried and ground, whitebait is used in soups. This recipe blends delicious fish with a piquant chile sauce, and can be served as part of a main course with vegetables and gari or rice, or as an accompaniment to drinks.*

SERVES 4

2 pounds (1 kg) whitebait or white sardines

2 teaspoons garlic salt

1 tablespoon hot paprika

1 tablespoon cornstarch

1 tablespoon peeled and grated fresh ginger

Vegetable oil, for deep-frying

PEPPER SAUCE

2 green onions, minced

4 cloves garlic, finely diced

10 fresh red chiles, minced

1 tablespoon peeled and grated fresh ginger

4 large tomatoes, finely diced

2 teaspoons shrimp paste or ½ cup ground dried shrimp

Salt

Wash the fish and dry with paper towels. Place in a bowl with the garlic salt, paprika, cornstarch and ginger. Mix well, making sure the fish is well coated.

Heat the vegetable oil in a large, deep skillet and deep-fry the fish in batches. Remove each batch as the fish becomes crispy and firm (fish must be crisp and crunchy, but be careful not to burn it). When the fish is cooked and ready, drain in a fine-mesh sieve lined with paper towels. Set aside and keep warm.

To make the sauce, fry the onions, garlic, chiles and ginger in approximately 2 tablespoons of the oil used to fry the fish. Fry until light brown. Add the tomatoes. Stir well and cook for approximately 10 minutes. Stir in the shrimp paste and simmer for 1 to 2 minutes. Remove from the heat and adjust the seasoning.

Serve the fish hot with the sauce in small bowls or plates for dipping. This dish can be accompanied by side dishes of rice or root vegetables or crudités of carrots, mushrooms, cauliflower, or zucchini.

NOTE: Alter quantities of chiles and tomatoes to taste.

African Risotto

This recipe, pronounced gahri fortor, *is based on* gari, *which is a coarse powder ground from the wonderful and versatile staple root vegetable of the African diet, the cassava. This is a kind of risotto that looks like the rice dish known as* jollof *(page 53) and could even be called gari jollof. Like rice,* gari *is the basis of many dishes; it is economical and high in fiber. And, again like rice, it swells to twice its original amount in water.*

Serve this dish at breakfast or as part of a main course at dinner. It has traveled across the world and is commonly eaten in Brazil (as farinhe de mandioca*), and in parts of the West Indies, such as Tobago.*

SERVES 4

1/2 cup vegetable oil

3 yellow or red onions, minced

2 fresh red chiles, minced (optional)

4 tomatoes, blanched, peeled, and finely diced

1 tablespoon tomato paste

1/2 cup cold water

Salt

Freshly ground black pepper

3/4 pound (375 g) *gari* (coarse cassava powder)

1 egg, scrambled without milk

1 head green-leaf or iceberg lettuce

2 extra tomatoes, sliced, for garnish

In a large, heavy-based saucepan, heat the oil and fry the onions and chiles until the onions are light brown.

Stir in the tomatoes and cook for 2 minutes. Add the tomato paste and water, and season with salt and pepper. Simmer for 4 to 5 minutes, stirring continuously to prevent burning.

Put the *gari* in a bowl. Add cold salted water to cover to the *gari* and let stand for 10 to 15 minutes, until the *gari* swells. Fluff out the *gari* with a fork, then add it, with the scrambled egg, to the onion and tomato sauce. Stir well to blend so the mixture turns pink.

Serve on lettuce leaves and garnish with tomatoes.

NOTE: *Eba* is a variation of this dish. To make *eba*, combine 1 1/2 cups *gari* with a pinch of salt and 2 cups of boiling water. The *gari* should absorb most of the water, but drain off any excess if necessary. Quickly knead into a firm, soft, smooth dough with a wooden spoon and form into rounds. Serve hot with stews and soups.

Black-Eyed Pea Pâté

Although the name might appear French, moi-moi is wholly Nigerian and is pronounced moy-moy. There are many variations on this pâté, which uses one of Africa's staple foods, beans, this time black-eyed peas. It is not only delicious, but it also has a wonderful contrasting texture of coarseness and smoothness. Serve it with a variety of fresh vegetables for a perfect light lunch or appetizer before dinner.

SERVES 4

2 cups dried black-eyed peas

2 cups cold water

Salt

1 yellow or white onion, minced

2 tablespoons vegetable oil

2 tablespoons tomato paste

1 egg

Freshly ground black pepper

Fresh parsley or vegetables, for garnish

Soak the black-eyed peas in water to cover overnight. Rinse and place in a medium pan with the cold water and a pinch of salt. Boil until the beans are nearly tender. Check regularly to ensure the pan does not boil dry. Drain all the water and cool the beans for about 20 minutes.

Place the boiled beans, onion, oil, tomato paste, egg, salt, and pepper to taste in a blender or food processor. Blend until thick and semi-smooth.

Pour into a greased steamer or microwave-safe dish, and cook until firm to the touch and coming away from the sides of the dish. If using a steamer, place over hot water for 25 to 30 minutes. Insert a skewer to check if the middle is cooked; if not, cook for a little longer. If you prefer to use a microwave, use a medium setting for 15 to 25 minutes.

Remove from the heat and cool for 10 to 15 minutes. Place a plate over the top of the dish, and tip the pâté onto the plate. Garnish with parsley, lettuce, mushrooms, tomatoes, or other vegetables of your choice.

Nigerian Sweet Puffs

POFF-POFF

My Ibo friend Rosarii and I had a good laugh at my efforts to translate the African name of this recipe, known in Nigeria as poff-poff, *a clear corruption of the English name puff-puff. Puff-puff describes the end result quite well, since these are puffed-up doughnuts. Extremely popular all over West Africa, their name changes from country to country. Back home in Ghana, they're referred to by the name* toogbei, *which literally translates to "sheeps' balls." For special occasions, food coloring is added to the batter to color the doughnuts, in which case they are called "the crown jewels."*

SERVES 4 TO 6

1/2 cup self-rising flour

1/2 cup all-purpose flour

1 teaspoon baking powder

2/3 cup superfine sugar, or to taste

1 teaspoon freshly grated nutmeg

2 teaspoons active dry yeast

1/2 to 3/4 cup water mixed with food coloring (optional)

Vegetable oil for deep-frying

Sift the flours and the baking powder together in a mixing bowl. Add the sugar, nutmeg, and yeast and mix in. Make a well in the center and stir in enough water and coloring to make a dough. Add small amounts of water at a time, so the dough is not too hard and not too soft. Cover and let stand for 1 hour to swell.

Using cupped fingers, scoop up small amounts of the dough to form small balls. Gently drop the balls of dough into a deep skillet of hot vegetable oil to deep-fry. The outside browns quickly; lower the heat immediately when the outside browns so the center can cook more slowly. Turn to brown both sides. When cooked, remove from the heat and drain on paper towels.

Serve hot or cold with other party foods and drink.

NOTE: Use the same dough to fry bigger doughnuts. However, bigger puffs are not considered as special for parties!

Chinchin

You can twist the sweet pastries made in this recipe into a variety of decorative shapes to serve as a treat on special occasions, particularly at Christmas. The puffs are common throughout West Africa and, like many traditional African dishes, have spread to the West Indies.

There are two methods for making the pastry: the rubbing method and the creaming method.

SERVES 4

RUBBING METHOD

2 cups flour

1 teaspoon baking powder

1/4 teaspoon salt

4 tablespoons butter

1/3 cup superfine sugar

1/2 teaspoon freshly grated nutmeg

1 to 2 beaten eggs

1/2 cup milk mixed with 1/4 cup cold water

Vegetable oil, for deep-frying

In a bowl, sift together the flour, baking powder, and salt. Rub in the butter. Add the sugar and nutmeg and make a well in the center.

Blend the eggs and the milk mixture together. Pour into well, and mix thoroughly by hand to form a pastry dough. On a lightly floured cutting board, roll out the pastry to an even thickness. Cut into 2-inch diamond shapes, and cut a slit in the middle of each diamond. Pull one diagonal end through the center slit.

Heat vegetable oil until it is very hot, and fry the pieces of twisted pastry until they are brown and cooked (try one first). Drain on paper towels and serve hot or cold.

CREAMING METHOD

4 tablespoons butter

2/3 cup superfine sugar

1 egg

2 tablespoons milk mixed with 2 tablespoons cold water

1/2 teaspoon freshly grated nutmeg

A dash of the flavoring of your choice (such as vanilla, banana, coconut, or rum)

Salt

1 teaspoon baking powder

4 tablespoons flour

Vegetable oil, for deep-frying

In a bowl, cream the butter and sugar together. Beat in the egg. Add the milk mixture, nutmeg, and flavoring of your choice. Set aside.

In another bowl, sift together the salt, baking powder, and flour. Add the egg-and-milk mixture and mix to form a firm dough. Roll out on a floured board, and proceed with cutting and frying as in rubbing method.

BRAZIL

OFFICIAL TITLE: República Federativa do Brasil

CAPITAL CITY: Brasília

OFFICIAL LANGUAGE: Portuguese, although English and French are spoken in business

CURRENCY: Brazilian Real = 100 centavos

CASH CROPS FOR EXPORT: Coffee, sugar, tobacco, cotton, sisal, rubber, jute, cassava, soybeans, cocoa beans, castor beans, bananas, oranges, carnauba wax, and nuts

FOOD CROPS: Corn, wheat, rice, sugar, soybeans, peanuts, some fruits, vegetables, livestock, and fish

TOTAL LAND AREA: 3,286,502 square miles

Black Bean Stew

Traditionally served in hotels in Rio de Janeiro for Saturday lunch, this black bean stew is generally considered Brazil's national dish. Feijoada has the longest list of ingredients I've ever seen and seems to use every leftover in the kitchen, but the result of this great variety of foods makes it absolutely unique and mouthwatering! This dish is excellent accompanied by white rice; peeled, sliced oranges; and finely shredded couvé *(see Note).*

SERVES 8

4 cups dried black beans or black-eyed peas

1 pound (500 g) dried beef or South African *biltong* (from a specialist butcher)

1 pound (500 g) salted pork

1 pound (500 g) pork spareribs (cured or smoked hock)

2 pig's feet

1/2 pound (250 g) salted pig's ear

2 chorizo, grilled and sliced, or 2 spicy Italian sausages

1 slice bacon

1 smoked beef tongue, cooked and sliced

2 tablespoons lard or butter

2 large yellow or white onions, diced

3 cloves garlic, crushed

6 to 10 green onions

1 bunch flat-leaf parsley

2 red bell peppers, seeded and diced

4 or 5 large tomatoes, blanched, peeled, and diced

1 bay leaf

Freshly ground black pepper

Chile powder, for seasoning

SPICY SAUCE

2 white onions, diced

3 fresh red chiles, minced

1 teaspoon cider vinegar

Juice of 2 to 3 lemons

Salt

2 green onions, chopped

1/2 cup olive oil

1/4 cup chopped fresh flat-leaf parsley

Soak the beans overnight in plenty of water. In a separate, large pan, soak the dried beef, salted pork, spareribs, pig's feet, and pig's ear in plenty of water overnight.

In a large pot, cook the beans in plenty of water. Drain the meats and cover with water again. Bring to a boil and boil for 1 minute. Drain and set aside. When the beans have cooked for 20 minutes, add the meats, the sausages, the bacon, and the tongue. Cook slowly, adding more water if necessary, and season with salt.

In a large pan, melt the lard. Sauté the yellow onions and garlic until the onions are golden. Tie the green onions and parsley together with kitchen twine to form a bouquet garni. Add the bell peppers, tomatoes, bay leaf, and bouquet garni, and season with pepper and chile powder.

Cook slowly on low heat for 20 minutes, then add 2 ladles of beans. Mash together well (avoiding the bouquet garni), then transfer to the remaining cooked beans and meat.

Stir everything together and continue cooking until the sauce thickens and the meats are tender and well cooked. Taste for seasoning and discard the bouquet garni.

To make the sauce, combine all the ingredients in a gravy-boat. Just before serving, add a ladleful of strained liquid from the stew.

Serve the bean stew and the cooked meats separately, with the sauce.

NOTE: *Couvé* is a green-leafed vegetable, and the best substitute is bok choy. However, if you are unable to find bok choy, use spinach or kale. Roll the leaves tightly and slice very thinly crosswise. Quickly stir-fry in a little bit of vegetable oil with crushed garlic. Season with salt and serve.

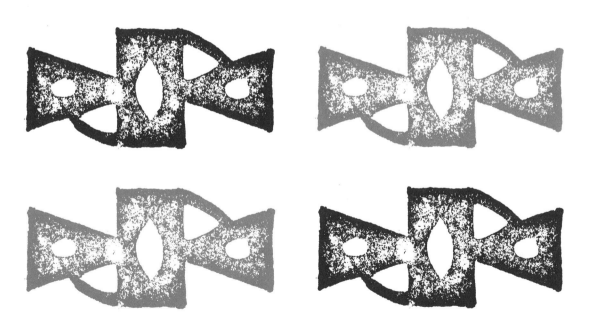

Black-eyed Pea and Shrimp Stew

The ubiquitous black-eyed pea is as widely traveled as the people who eat it. Appearing here in a Brazilian dish, it is also a staple dietary item in many regions of Africa due to its importance as an inexpensive and long-lasting secondary protein. Wherever African food has traveled, black-eyed peas have been part of the luggage! Serve this stew with grilled or fried plantains (page 202), and boiled brown or white rice.

SERVES 4

4 cups dried black-eyed peas

Salt

1 cup palm or dende oil

3 large yellow onions, cut into thin strips

3 tomatoes, blanched, peeled, and diced

2 to 3 fresh red chiles, diced (optional)

1 cup dried shrimp

Soak the black-eyed peas in plenty of water overnight. Rinse the beans well with fresh water, then boil them in a large pan, with plenty of water and a pinch of salt. Cook for 30 to 40 minutes, or until the beans are soft but not mushy. Drain the beans and set them aside.

In a separate, large cooking pot, heat the oil. Sauté the onions until just golden. Add the tomatoes and chiles, stirring well to prevent burning. Cook for about 3 minutes on medium heat, stirring continuously. Add the dried shrimp and stir. Decrease the heat and cook for 3 more minutes. Stir in the cooked beans, and simmer for 10 to 15 minutes before serving.

Shrimp Stew

This Brazilian dish is so similar in many ways to a Ghanaian okra stew (page 12) that I feel sure it is one of the recipes carried west from Africa during the slave trade and modified over generations to suit the new local conditions. Like most African stews, it is best served with gari *or rice.*

SERVES 4

2 pounds (1 kg) fresh shrimp

3 tablespoons olive oil

2 cloves garlic, diced

2 yellow onions, grated

4 tomatoes, chopped

1 green bell pepper, seeded and diced

1²/3 cups coconut milk

1 pound (500 g) dried shrimp

2 tablespoons palm oil, or to taste

2 pounds (1 kg) okra, topped, tailed, and cut into 1-inch pieces

Chopped fresh green chiles

Wash and peel the fresh shrimp in a bowl of warm water; reserve the water. In a large skillet, heat the olive oil and gently fry the garlic, onions, tomatoes, and bell pepper. Add the fresh shrimp and cook for 10 minutes. Add the coconut milk, dried shrimp, and palm oil. Continue cooking for 10 to 15 minutes, or until the stew has thickened.

Cook the okra in the reserved shrimp water until soft. When cooked, drain the okra and mix it with the shrimp mixture. Season with the chiles to taste.

Serve hot.

Brazilian Chicken and Peanut Stew

VATAPA

This Bahian dish is another that I am sure had its origins in West Africa. It is similar to nkatsebe, *the peanut and palmnut stew that is popular in the Akan region of Ghana. Serve it with steamed rice and baked sweet potatoes.*

Bahia is situated on the northeastern coast of Brazil, and it is the country's most African state; most of its inhabitants can trace their origins through the slave trade to West Africa, particularly Nigeria.

SERVES 6 TO 8

12 to 15 cloves garlic, crushed

Salt

Freshly ground black pepper

1 chicken, 4 pounds (2 kg), cut into serving pieces

Olive oil, for frying

6 cups cold water

1 large red onion, grated

2 bunches cilantro

Chopped fresh red chiles

1 pound (500 g) dried shrimp, soaked in water for 12 hours, or ½ cup shrimp paste

1 cup peanut paste or peanut butter

2 tablespoons *farinhe de mandioca* (coarse cassava powder)

2 cups coconut milk mixed with 1 cup cold water

1 cup palm oil

Marinate the chicken in half the crushed garlic, salt, and pepper. In a large skillet, heat the olive oil and add the chicken pieces. Add the water and cook the chicken for 20 minutes, or until tender. Remove the bones and set the meat aside. Leave the stock in the skillet. Add the remaining garlic, onion, cilantro, and chiles. Bring to a boil.

Drain the shrimp and mince them. In a bowl, mix the peanut paste with the *farinhe de mandioca*. Add the minced shrimp, the peanut paste mixture, and the coconut milk mixture to the stock.

Stir continuously for 2 to 3 minutes, or until the stock thickens. Add the chicken meat and the palm oil. Gently simmer for 3 to 4 minutes, stirring regularly to prevent sticking or burning.

Serve hot.

NOTE: You can substitute fish for chicken.

If you have any difficulty finding palm oil, use another vegetable oil and add 4 tablespoons ground turmeric to it.

Bobo of Shrimp

This is a most unusual way to cook shrimp. The palm oil and cassava signal that the recipe is of African origin, but the method shows a Portuguese influence—the blend of two cultures create a unique flavor.

SERVES 4 TO 6

2 pounds (1 kg) cassava, peeled and diced

2 cups coconut milk mixed with 1/2 teaspoon salt

4 tablespoons olive oil

2 yellow onions, diced

4 tomatoes, chopped

1 clove garlic, diced

1 bunch cilantro, chopped

2 pounds shrimp, peeled and deveined, with tails intact

2 tablespoons palm oil

Chopped fresh red chiles, for seasoning

Salt

Boil the cassava in a small amount of water flavored with 2 to 3 tablespoons of the salted coconut milk for 25 minutes, until the cassava is soft. Divide the cassava into 2 portions, and put one through a blender or food processor.

In a large skillet, heat the olive oil and sauté the onions, tomatoes, garlic, and cilantro for about 5 minutes. Add the shrimp and gently simmer for 5 to 7 minutes, or until the shrimp is opaque.

Add the blended cassava, the diced cassava, the remaining coconut milk, and the palm oil. Season with chiles and salt. Serve with steamed rice.

NOTE: If you have difficulty finding palm oil, use another vegetable oil and add 1 tablespoon turmeric to it.

Bahia

Bahia is a region on the northeast coast of Brazil that still maintains strong cultural ties to West Africa, particularly Nigeria.

Discovered in 1501 by early Portuguese explorers, the region was originally called Bahia de Todos os Santos, or All Saints Bay. The Portuguese brought in indentured labor from Africa to build their colonies in South America.

The Africans and the Amerindians have coexisted in compromise ever since, maintaining certain separate cultural and religious activities, but blending in the necessities of day-to-day life.

Invoking the Spirits

The African influence on Brazil appears most striking in worship and related dance and music. The strong Nigerian origins can be traced through the continued worship in both name and practice of Ogun, Obatala, Shango, and other Nigerian tribal gods.

While most slaves were forced to convert to Christianity, a number of original beliefs and customs were preserved.

Although some customs survived intact, others became mixed with elements of Christian belief and evolved into forms of worship that became distinctive in particular regions: thus *candomblé, macumba* and *unganda* in Brazil; *shango* in Trinidad; *santeria* in Cuba; and voodoo in Haiti. Contrary to popular belief, voodoo is not an African form of witchcraft, but a hybrid form of worship.

All the religions involve some form of ritualistic African-style drum music to invoke the spirits' participation. The ceremonies often culminate in trancelike dancing, during which the followers are apparently possessed by the deity. Frequently, the "possessed" dance until they collapse from exhaustion.

It is said that the Brazilian samba and the Cuban rumba have their origins in these dances.

Chin-Chin of Chicken

This is yet another recipe that shows its African beginnings. To this day a similar recipe that uses fish instead of chicken is cooked in Ghana, where it is served with cornmeal dumplings such as banku *(page 21) instead of rice. Since this is a Brazilian dish, it is most often served with rice.*

SERVES 6 TO 8

1 chicken, 4 pounds (2 kg)

Salt

6 to 8 cloves garlic, crushed

1/2 cup olive oil

1 tablespoon palm or dende oil

1 tablespoon peeled and grated fresh ginger

2 yellow onions, minced

1/2 cup ground dried shrimp

Cut the chicken into serving pieces. Season with salt and garlic, and marinate in the refrigerator for at least 2 hours, preferably longer.

In a large skillet, heat the olive oil and fry the chicken pieces until they turn golden. Drain excess oil, and add the palm oil, ginger, onions, and shrimp. Cook gently for 20 to 30 minutes, or until the chicken is tender. You may need to add some water to prevent burning. Add small amounts of hot water, because this dish needs to be reasonably dry.

Serve hot.

A Culinary Departure

The links to West Africa are still strong in Bahia, not only in religion and dress (many black women still dress as their African counterparts do), but also in food, although the Portuguese have strongly influenced Bahian cuisine.

Like the West Africans, Bahians favor palm oil (called *dende* oil in Brazil), beans, and coarse cassava powder (called *gari* in West Africa, but *farinhe de mandioca* in Brazil) in many of their recipes. Some dishes are almost identical, such as the Bahian fish dish called *moquecan*, which is prepared in virtually the same way as West African fish recipes and is even served with a similar sauce made from chiles and palm oil.

While the origins are obvious, Bahian cuisine does show what can evolve over distance and time. For example, in African cooking chiles and herbs are added during preparation, while in Bahia these flavorings are added last. Also, the use of coconut milk, spices, and even fruits—mixing the sweet with the savory—shows a departure from traditional African cuisine.

Chocolate Pot

It should come as no surprise that I have included a chocolate recipe in this book. I was born and bred in Ghana, a country that, like Brazil, was for many years a leader in the growing and export of cocoa beans to the chocolate-mad world, but I grew up not liking chocolate! No, not all chocolate—just the cheap, very sweet and sickly variety. My point is that if you must eat chocolate, eat only the best—hence my Chocolate Pot recipe. It's smooth, dark, and mysterious and made with the very best chocolate. I should be named "Miss Chocolate"!

SERVES 8

16 ounces (500 g) high-quality bittersweet chocolate

2 cups heavy cream

1/4 teaspoon almond extract

1/4 teaspoon vanilla extract

4 egg yolks, lightly beaten with a fork

4 tablespoons butter, melted and warm (optional)

1 cup Frangelico (hazelnut liqueur)

Break the chocolate into small pieces by hand, and place in the top pan of a double boiler or in a medium, heavy-based pan. Rest this pan inside another, larger pan or cooking pot that is one-third full of boiling water. Place over medium heat so the water in the base pan stays at a gentle boil.

Melt the chocolate in the top pan, making sure there is always sufficient water in the base pan and that no water gets into the top pan.

Using a wooden spoon, stir the chocolate until fully melted; do not boil. Whisk in the cream and the extracts and mix well. Add the egg yolks and continue to whisk firmly but smoothly until all is mixed. Add the melted butter (it must not be too hot) for a final, shiny glaze.

Pour the mixture into 8 3-ounce ramekins, filling them only two-thirds full. Arrange all the ramekins on a tray and place them in the refrigerator for 15 to 20 minutes to firm lightly (but not too hard).

To serve, pour 2 tablespoons of Frangelico on top of each dessert. Serve alone or accompanied by Drunken Oranges (page 30).

TRINIDAD AND TOBAGO

OFFICIAL TITLE: Republic of Trinidad and Tobago

CAPITAL CITY: Port of Spain

OFFICIAL LANGUAGE: English, although French, Spanish, Hindi, and Chinese are spoken

CURRENCY: Trinidad and Tobago dollar (TT$) = 100 cents

CASH CROPS FOR EXPORT: Sugar, coffee, cocoa, coconuts, and fresh fruits

FOOD CROPS: Sugar, beans, sweet potatoes, vegetables, coconuts, and fruit

TOTAL LAND AREA: Trinidad: 1,864 square miles; Tobago: 116 square miles

Spinach Soup

Callaloo is the Trinidadian name for a soup based on a variety of spinach known locally as dasheen. *You may substitute spinach. This soup is usually part of the tradition of Sunday feasting after going to church.*

SERVES 4

1 bunch spinach, minced
(including stems)

1 pig's tail, or 3 ounces (90 g)
salted pork, cut into small
pieces

1 cup coconut milk

6 1/3 cups cold water

1 onion, diced

2 cloves garlic

2 medium crabs, or 1/2 pound
(250 g) crabmeat

1/2 pound (250 g) okra, topped,
tailed, and cut into 1-inch
pieces

Salt

Freshly ground black pepper

Trinidadian Dumplings
(page 165)

Place the *dasheen*, pig's tail, coconut milk, water, onion, and garlic in a large soup pot, and simmer on low heat for about 10 minutes, or until the pig's tail is tender. If you are using live crabs, add them with those ingredients. When the meat is tender, add the okra and crabmeat (if you aren't using live crabs). Season with salt and pepper and simmer until the okra seeds become darkish pink and the soup is thick.

Serve hot with the dumplings.

The Land of the Hummingbird

It was only on Christopher Columbus's third voyage to the Caribbean region that he discovered Trinidad in 1498. This small island and its even smaller satellite, Tobago, lie between the southern tail of the Windward group of islands and the coast of Venezuela. The islands are separated by just a few kilometers from Venezuela by two sea channels: Dragon's Mouth and Serpent's Mouth.

Trinidad was originally called *Lere* or "the land of the hummingbird" by its Amerindian inhabitants.

Saltfish Salad

This fish salad is usually eaten with Bake Flat Bread (page 164), a breadlike biscuit. I have been told by my Trinidadian friend Annette Holton about a shop in San Fernando owned by old Mrs. Tuckoor (affectionately known as Mummy Daph), for which workmen made a beeline every morning to buy their daily bake *and* buljol.

SERVES 4 TO 6

1 pound (500 g) dried salted fish

1 yellow onion, diced

1/2 red bell pepper, seeded and finely diced

1/2 green bell pepper, seeded and finely diced

2 tomatoes, diced

1 teaspoon fresh lemon thyme

1/2 Scotch bonnet chile, or 1 fresh red chile, seeded and finely diced

1 tablespoon chopped fresh chives

2 or 3 cloves garlic, very finely diced

Freshly ground black pepper

1/4 cup olive oil

2 tablespoons freshly squeezed lime juice

Trinidadian Flat Bread (page 164)

In a pan, soak the salted fish in boiling water to remove excess salt, changing the water several times. When all the salt has been removed, shred the fish and remove any excess water and the bones. Place the shredded fish in a bowl, and mix with the onion, bell peppers, tomatoes, thyme, chile, chives, and garlic, and season with pepper.

Cover and set aside for about 10 minutes. Stir in the olive oil and lime juice to give a nice, moist, finishing touch. Cover and refrigerate, preferably overnight, so that all the flavors can permeate the fish. Remove from the refrigerator and bring to room temperature. Serve with the bread.

NOTE: As a variation, add chopped mushrooms and cubed ripe avocados to the salad mixture just before serving.

Trinidadian Flat Bread

There are three traditional ways to cook this Trinidadian and Tobagonian flat bread: you can fry it, bake it, or grill it, generally on a coalpot or griddle. Mummy Daph (page 163) used to make bakes *to go with* buljol *on the top of a coalpot. A coalpot is like a small coal-fired barbecue, but Western cooks can use oil in a skillet.*

SERVES 4 TO 6

1 teaspoon superfine sugar

1/2 cup lukewarm water

2 teaspoons active dry yeast

1/2 cup coconut milk

1/4 teaspoon salt

4 tablespoons butter, melted

2 cups flour, sifted

Vegetable oil, for cooking

Stir the sugar into the lukewarm water, and soak the yeast in this for 5 minutes. Stir to dissolve. Mix the coconut milk with the salt and melted butter in a large mixing bowl. Gradually add the frothy yeast mixture, and stir in the sifted flour until a soft dough forms.

Add more flour in small amounts if necessary. Knead the dough for about 3 minutes, or until it is elastic and smooth. Cover the bowl and let stand in a warm place for 30 minutes to rise.

Transfer the risen dough to a floured board. Lightly knead the dough and form it into small, even dough balls. Return to the bowl. Cover and let stand in a warm place for 15 minutes.

Flatten into rounds of desired size with a floured rolling pin.

Lightly grease a skillet with vegetable oil, heat over medium heat, and add the flattened dough rounds in batches.

Cook, turning to ensure even cooking, for 2 to 3 minutes on medium heat, or until cooked through and lightly golden on both sides. Remove from the skillet and cover with a clean, folded dish towel to keep warm until all the dough rounds are cooked.

Trinidadian Dumplings

These dumplings are popular in the West Indies where the recipes vary depending on whether the dumplings will accompany a soup or a stew. This particular version is meant to go with soups such as callaloo (page 162).

SERVES 4

¼ cup flour

¼ cup cornmeal

Salt

2 teaspoons baking powder

1 teaspoon fresh herb or spice of choice (optional)

1 tablespoon butter

In a bowl, mix the flours with the salt, baking powder, and herbs. Thoroughly rub in the butter. Gradually add very small amounts of water until the flour becomes a soft dough.

Break off small pieces of dough, and roll them into finger-size shapes. Drop these shapes into the soup to cook.

NOTE: Some people prefer to make their dumplings plain by omitting the butter and baking powder. Alternatively, make more elaborate dumplings by including numerous herbs and spices such as ground allspice, freshly grated nutmeg, crushed dried red chiles, finely chopped fresh basil, and so forth.

Steamed Cornmeal

COOCOO

There are innumerable ways to prepare steamed cornmeal—it all depends from which island you take the recipe; this one is from Tobago. One thing that all the recipes for steamed cornmeal have in common is that they are derived from the African version, variously known as banku, ugali, sadza, mealie-meal, *and* nsima, *among others. On the islands, this is often served with fried, steamed, or baked fish.*

SERVES 4

Salt

7 1/2 cups cold water

10 to 16 okra pods, topped, tailed, and sliced into thick rings

4 tablespoons butter

1 1/2 cups cornmeal

Sliced tomatoes, for garnish

Sliced green bell peppers, for garnish

Chopped fresh flat-leaf parsley, for garnish

In a large pot, add some salt to the water and bring to a boil. Add the okra and 2 tablespoons of the butter. Slowly pour in the cornmeal, stirring constantly to prevent lumps. Decrease the heat and continue stirring for 15 to 20 minutes, or until the cornmeal absorbs most of the water and is cooked.

Grease a serving dish with the remaining butter. Tip the cornmeal mixture into the dish, and swirl it about to form a ball. Garnish with the tomatoes, bell peppers, and parsley.

Serve hot.

NOTE: In Trinidad, 1/2 cup cooked corn kernels is often added to *coocoo*.

Pigeon Peas and Rice

PELAU

Pelau is a popular dish throughout the Caribbean, often served with stews and roasts. Pigeon peas (also known in Jamaica as gungo peas) are actually beans, not peas, and are of African origin. You can buy pigeon peas fresh or dried. The amounts of the herbs can be adjusted according to taste.

SERVES 4

¼ cup vegetable oil

1 tablespoon brown sugar

1 pound (500 g) boneless beef or chicken, cut into chunks

1 cup long-grain white rice

1 cup dried pigeon peas or black-eyed peas

½ cup coconut milk

2 cups water

Salt

Freshly ground black pepper

4 cloves garlic, minced

½ cup chopped fresh parsley

1 red onion, minced

½ teaspoon salt

2 tablespoons chopped fresh chives

In a large cooking pot, heat the oil. Add the brown sugar and stir until it has almost caramelized. Add the meat or chicken with a little water, and simmer until the meat is half cooked. Stir in the rice, pigeon peas, coconut milk, water, garlic, parsley, onion, salt, and chives and season with salt and pepper. Simmer on low heat for 20 to 25 minutes, or until everything is cooked and moist but not soggy.

Serve hot.

Lemon-Ginger Fish

This tasty recipe is delightful with whole fish, but you can also use steaks or fillets. The flavorful sauce adds another dimension of flavors to the tasty fish. Serve this dish with steamed jasmine rice.

SERVES 4 TO 6

1¹/₂ pounds (750 g) whole fish (such as snapper, mackerel, or porgy), cleaned and scaled

1 tablespoon peeled and very finely grated fresh ginger

2 tablespoons lemon thyme

1 tablespoon olive oil

Sea salt

Freshly ground black pepper

SAUCE

2 tablespoons olive oil

3 green onions, minced

2 cloves garlic, minced

1 tablespoon peeled and finely grated fresh ginger

3 button mushrooms, cleaned and sliced into very thin strips

1¹/₂ tablespoons superfine sugar

1 tablespoon ground turmeric

2 teaspoons tamarind paste blended with 1 tablespoon hot water

2 cups vegetable stock

1 tablespoon fish sauce

Salt

Freshly ground black pepper

¹/₄ red bell pepper, seeded and sliced into thin strips

¹/₄ yellow bell pepper, seeded and sliced into thin strips

¹/₄ green bell pepper, seeded and sliced into thin strips

1 small red onion, sliced into thin strips

1 tablespoon cornstarch blended with 2 tablespoons cold water

Cilantro sprigs, for garnish

Flat-leaf parsley sprigs, for garnish

Preheat the oven to 350°F/180°C.

Have your fishmonger scale and clean the fish, as well as trim off the fins and tail.

Place the fish on a chopping board, and dry with a paper towel. Using a sharp knife, carefully make 2 deep, diagonal cuts (about ³/4 inch apart) across the full length of the fish in the fleshy part. Repeat the same cuts traveling in the opposite direction to form a crisscross pattern on the fish. Do not cut down to the bone. Turn the fish over and repeat the same pattern of cuts.

Mix together the ginger, lemon thyme, and olive oil, and season with salt and pepper. Stuff the seasoning into the cuts on both sides, making sure that every cut is well filled with the seasoning. Rub any remaining seasoning on the body of the fish and into the head.

Grease a sheet of foil. Loosely wrap the seasoned fish and bake for about 20 to 30 minutes, or until the fish flakes when tested with a fork. While the fish is baking, prepare the sauce.

To make the sauce, heat the oil in a large skillet and sauté the green onions, garlic, ginger, and mushrooms over low to medium heat for about 5 minutes. Add the sugar and continue to cook for 3 minutes.

Stir in the turmeric, tamarind paste, vegetable stock, and fish sauce. Taste and season with salt and pepper. Continue cooking on low heat for 5 minutes. Add the red, yellow, and green bell peppers and the onion, and cook for approximately 3 minutes. Mix in the cornstarch and stir until the sauce thickens.

Pour the juices from the baked fish into the pan and stir to mix. Arrange the baked fish on a large plate, and spoon the sauce over it. Garnish with the parsley and cilantro.

Serve immediately.

Carnival

Carnival has a long history in Trinidad. The tradition was brought to the island by the French sugarcane planters who escaped slave uprisings on the French island colonies of Martinique and Haiti in the mid-eighteenth century.

The original celebrations, which lasted from Christmas to Ash Wednesday, excluded the black slaves. The French plantation owners painted their faces black, dressed up as field slaves (*negré jardin*), and danced to African drum rhythms. The slaves only participated to provide entertainment for their owners.

The abolition of the slave trade in 1834 freed the slaves to celebrate their own Carnival. Drawing on their ancestral West African traditions, well-known figures and rituals such as Shango, Mama Deleau (Mami Water in Ghana), the Kalinda stick dance, and Bamboula became integral to the festivities. These were added to the European rituals to create the spectacular annual Carnival shows held today.

T *and* T

Trinidad was initially colonized by the Spanish, who had control for almost three hundred years, although French and Dutch settlements periodically sprang up during this time. Power of the island was wrested from the Spanish by the British in 1797 during the Napoleonic wars. Neighboring Tobago changed hands among the Spanish, British, French, and Dutch many times in just over two hundred years. Finally, in 1888, Tobago became a ward of Trinidad.

All the colonialists were eager to exploit the fertile terrain and excellent climate. African slave labor was used until the trade was abolished in 1834, when indentured labor from India and Asia was brought in to work on the estates, all adding to the extraordinarily diverse racial and cultural mix that still makes up "T and T's" population today.

Calypso

A uniquely Trinidadian form of music, calypso evolved from the drum rhythms brought from Africa during the slave trade and the melodic influence of French and Spanish colonizers. The lyric element of calypso first derived from the folk chant of the West African people, but it soon developed into long and taunting songs that satirized their colonial masters, passed on gossip, and unified the people's sense of identity.

Steel bands are an integral part of calypso and originated in Trinidad, too. Also evolving from the African drum heritage, metal drums were used when, under British rule, African drums were banned. The metal containers are cut into various sizes to produce different pitches and then hammered into sections to allow separate notes to sound. So sophisticated are steel drums today that practically any style of music can be played on them.

Melons in Coconut Rum

I'm told watermelon has its origins in South Africa, so I feel suitably proud to produce this fun melon recipe in honor of the humble but delicious ruby red watermelon and her European melon friends! Rum is made on the islands, and pairs extremely well with melon.

SERVES 4

MELON BALLS

½ seedless watermelon

½ cantaloupe, seeded

½ ripe honeydew melon, seeded

½ ripe Crenshaw melon, seeded

COCONUT RUM

6 tablespoons good-quality white rum

1 cup fresh pineapple juice

¼ cup coconut milk

2 tablespoons coconut liqueur (such as Malibu)

2 tablespoons simple syrup

Soak 12 small to medium wooden skewers in cold water for about 1 hour. Using a melon baller, scoop out balls from each type of melon. Spear the balls onto the skewers, alternating the melon types. Allow for 4 to 6 balls per skewer until all the balls are used.

Arrange the skewers of melons on a deep serving platter.

Combine all the ingredients for the coconut rum in a blender or cocktail shaker. Blend or shake well to mix thoroughly. Strain through a fine-mesh sieve, and pour evenly over the prepared melon balls. Serve immediately or cover and chill for 1 or 2 hours before serving.

MARTINIQUE AND GUADELOUPE

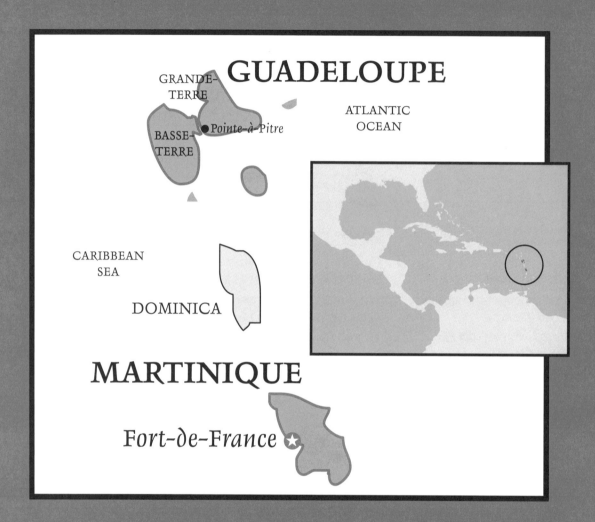

OFFICIAL TITLE: Martinique and Guadeloupe

CAPITAL CITY: Fort-de-France (Martinique) and Basse-Terre (Guadeloupe)

OFFICIAL LANGUAGE: French, although English and Creole are spoken

CURRENCY: French franc (FF) = 100 centimes

CASH CROPS FOR EXPORT: Sugar, bananas, and pineapples

FOOD CROPS: Sugar, rice, fresh fruits, vegetables, livestock, and fish

TOTAL LAND AREA: Martinique: 425 square miles; Guadeloupe: 687 square miles

Ratatouille Créole

This dish reminds me of Zimbabwean cucumber and pumpkin dishes. Although cucumber is not generally eaten in other African countries, it is sometimes used in vegetable stews, depending on local availability. Cucumber is common to Martinique and Guadeloupe, however, and lends itself beautifully to the ratatouille.

SERVES 4 TO 6

3/4 cup olive oil

2 yellow onions, sliced into thin rings

2 red sweet or bell peppers, seeded and sliced into wide strips

2 green sweet or bell peppers, seeded and sliced into wide strips

1 pound zucchini, chopped

2 large cucumbers, peeled and thickly sliced

2 eggplants, peeled and chopped

4 tomatoes, blanched, peeled, and thickly sliced

Salt

Freshly ground black pepper

1 teaspoon dried mixed herbs

Sugar, for seasoning (optional)

Preheat the oven to 400°F/200°C.

Pour the olive oil into a very large ovenproof dish, add the onions, cover, and bake for 10 minutes. Remove from the oven. In layers on top of the onions, arrange attractively the red and green peppers, zucchini, cucumbers, eggplants, and tomatoes. Season with salt and pepper.

Cover and return to the oven for 10 minutes. Uncover and add the herbs and sugar. Continue baking for 20 to 30 minutes, or until all the ingredients are cooked and any juices have reduced. This dish must be moist, not dry.

Serve hot alone or as an accompaniment to baked or roasted fish or meat dishes.

Shrimp, Avocado, and Mango Salad

One of the things that excites me most about Caribbean cuisine is the custom of combining exotic fruits and vegetables with seafood for delicious dishes. It is a concept alien to my early upbringing, but one which I've nonetheless come to love. This salad is one of my favorites.

SERVES 4

2 pounds (1 kg) large fresh shrimp, cooked, peeled, and deveined, with tails intact

1 yellow onion, minced

Juice of 3 lemons

1 tablespoon olive oil

2 tablespoons sweet chile sauce

1 tablespoon balsamic vinegar

1 clove garlic, minced

2 large avocados

Salt

Freshly ground black pepper

2 firm, ripe mangoes, peeled and thinly sliced

1 medium bunch cilantro, minced

Bread, as accompaniment

Make sure the shrimp are well cleaned, heads discarded, and peeled. Carefully rinse them under cold running water. Dab with paper towels to dry. Check that each prawn is deveined, then carefully cut each vertically down the center into 2 equal halves. Cover and set aside.

To make the dressing, in a medium bowl, combine the onion with the juice of 1 lemon, the oil, sweet chile sauce, balsamic vinegar, and garlic. Stir well to mix and let stand for about 30 minutes.

Peel the avocados and carefully cut them into 1-inch cubes. Douse them liberally with the juice of 2 lemons and season with salt and pepper. Cover and let stand for about 5 minutes.

Using a slotted spoon, remove the avocado cubes from the lemon marinade, and arrange them in a salad bowl. Arrange the shrimp on top, followed by the slices of ripe mango. Drizzle the salad with the onion dressing and very carefully stir to mix thoroughly without crushing or disturbing the avocados and shrimp too much. Taste and adjust the seasoning. Sprinkle with the cilantro.

Serve immediately with your favorite bread.

Baby Plantains in Sauce

JEUNES BANANES AUX SAUCES

Just as in Africa, plantains are a favorite of the French Caribbean, although more often than not they are treated as a sweet rather than a savory. Acting contrary to custom, I chose this savory plantain recipe from Martinique.

SERVES 4

4 to 8 unripe baby plantains

Salt

½ cup butter

3 to 4 tablespoons flour

1½ cups milk

Freshly ground black pepper

½ cup grated Parmesan or other hard, dry cheese

1 teaspoon freshly grated nutmeg

Preheat the oven to 400°F/200°C.

Lightly oil your hands to prevent the plantain juice from staining them. Score the plantains lengthwise with a sharp knife. Peel off the green skins, and extract the baby plantains whole.

Rinse and place the plantains in a large pan. Cover with cold water, sprinkle with salt, and bring to a boil. Cook for 15 to 20 minutes, or until the plantains soften. Remove from the heat and drain off the water. Arrange the cooked plantains in a large, deep, buttered ovenproof dish; set aside and keep warm.

In a deep skillet, melt the butter over low heat. Stir in the flour and mix well to form a roux. Pour in the milk and stir continuously until it thickens into a smooth white sauce. Season with salt and pepper. Pour evenly over the plantains to cover, top with the grated cheese, and sprinkle nutmeg over the top. Bake, uncovered, for 10 to 15 minutes.

Serve as hot as you wish.

Rice and Peas, Guadeloupe Style

POIS ROUGES MACONNE

Rice and peas is nearly synonymous with the West Indies, and each island has its own special way of cooking the dish. This recipe from Guadeloupe is different from any other rice-and-pea combinations I have come across. Actually, the combination is of rice and beans, but for some unknown reason it is called rice and peas all over the Caribbean. Apart from the intrigue with the name, I discovered that it originated from the gari and bean dishes of Africa, but had evolved with tasty additions of bacon, garlic, and rice. I have been hooked ever since.

SERVES 4

¹/₄ cup peanut oil

1 large yellow onion, diced

2 cloves garlic, diced

1 to 2 fresh red chiles, diced

4 slices bacon, chopped

2¹/₄ cups dried red kidney beans, soaked in water for 1 hour, then drained and rinsed

4¹/₄ cups cold water

Salt

Freshly ground black pepper

1 cup long-grain rice

2 tablespoons *farine de manioc* (coarse cassava powder)

In a large pan, heat the oil and gently sauté the onion, garlic, chiles, and bacon until the bacon is cooked but not browned. Add the beans and water and season with salt and pepper. Bring to a boil and simmer for 45 minutes to 1 hour, or until the beans are half-cooked. Add the rice, and stir well to mix. Cover and simmer on very low heat until both the rice and beans are cooked and soft. You may need to add more water at this stage to help the rice cook if there is not enough, but be careful not to make it too soggy.

Stir in the *farine de manioc* to absorb any remaining fluid and to thicken the sauce. Adjust the seasoning and leave on very low heat for 5 minutes before serving.

Serve hot.

Escargots

Snails are very popular in West Africa, where they grow to phenomenal sizes in the rain forests. The biggest snails come from the Ivory Coast. They are used fresh in soups and vegetable stews or are dried and salted to preserve them for eating later in the season when fresh snails are scarce. This recipe from Martinique and Guadeloupe is a very French way of preparing snails. Serve the escargots with boiled long-grain rice and fresh green vegetables of your choice.

SERVES 4

Salt

6 cups water

8 to 12 fresh snails, or
  1 1-pound (500-g) can
  snails

1/2 cup butter

2 green onions, diced

3 cloves garlic, diced

2 to 4 fresh red chiles, diced,
  or 1 teaspoon hot paprika

1/2 pound (250 g) button
  mushrooms, cleaned and
  quartered

1/2 pound (250 g) spinach,
  very finely sliced

Salt

Freshly ground black pepper

1 cup heavy cream

If using fresh snails, add the salt to the water in a large pan and bring to a boil. Drop in the snails and cook for 20 to 30 minutes, or until the flesh is tender and cooked. Drain the snails and soak in cold water for 10 minutes to cool. Remove their shells and pull off the entrails and all the slimy attachments from the main black body. Cut each cleaned snail into half down the full length of its body. If you are using canned snails, open the can, drain them, and cut each one into half down the full length of its body.

In a large cooking pot, melt the butter and sauté the onions, garlic, chiles, and mushrooms for 10 to 15 minutes. Add the snails and spinach and cook for 10 to 15 minutes, stirring continuously. Season with salt and pepper and stir in the cream. Cook for 5 to 10 minutes, or until the sauce has thickened slightly.

Serve hot.

French Caribbean Crab Risotto

This is another West Indian dish in which you can easily recognize the African ancestry. It is like the seafood or crab jollof *rice found in Sierra Leone or Liberia or a* gari *and crab dish that is favored in Ghana, Togo, Benin, and Nigeria.*

This recipe is from Guadeloupe and is cooked very quickly with spices in the French way.

SERVES 4

2/3 cup olive oil

2 pounds (1 kg) crabmeat

2 large yellow or white
    onions, diced

4 cloves garlic, diced

2 to 3 fresh red chiles, diced

Herbs (such as oregano,
    thyme, or chives) (optional)

Salt

1½ cups long-grain white rice

2 or 3 bay leaves

4¼ cups hot vegetable stock
    or 4 cups hot water mixed
    with 2 crushed vegetable
    bouillon cubes

Red leaf lettuce leaves,
    for garnish

Hard-boiled eggs, sliced, for
    garnish (optional)

Cucumber and tomato slices,
    for garnish (optional)

Chopped fresh chives,
    for garnish

Juice of 1 lemon

In a large, heavy-based pan, heat the oil and toss in the crabmeat, onions, garlic, chiles, and herbs. Season with salt. Cook over medium heat, stirring continuously, for 5 to 10 minutes, being careful not to let the crabmeat break up. Add the rice, bay leaves, and vegetable stock. Adjust the seasoning to taste. Cover and cook on very low heat for 20 to 30 minutes, or until the rice is cooked and absorbs all the water. You may need to add more water, depending on the type of rice. Remove the bay leaves before serving.

Serve hot arranged on lettuce leaves, garnished with either sliced hard-boiled eggs or a mixture of sliced cucumbers and tomatoes, and topped with chopped chives and lemon juice.

Sautéed Chicken in Coconut Milk

SAUTÉ DE POULET AU COCO

Chicken and coconut dishes lend themselves to individual touches. This is the basic recipe from Martinique and Guadeloupe, but feel free to experiment: add some wine or lime juice—who knows, you may discover an inspired version!

SERVES 4

4 to 6 chicken pieces (breasts, wings, or thighs), or 6 to 8 drumsticks

1/4 cup flour mixed with 1 tablespoon salt

1 cup vegetable oil

2 1/4 cups coconut milk

1 yellow onion, diced

2 cloves red garlic, diced

1/2 pound (250 g) whole button or small mushrooms, cleaned

2 fresh red chiles, diced (optional)

Garlic or celery salt, for seasoning (optional)

4 cups hot boiled long-grain white rice

2 tomatoes, sliced

Rinse the chicken and dry with paper towels. Season with the flour-salt mixture. Heat the oil in a large skillet, and fry the chicken until golden. Remove from the heat, and pour the excess oil into a separate skillet; set aside.

Return the chicken pieces to the stove in the same skillet without rinsing it—the browned base retains the chicken juices and adds flavor. Add the coconut milk and simmer on very low heat. Using the leftover oil, sauté the onion, red garlic, mushrooms, and chiles until the onions soften and brown. Add to the chicken simmering in the coconut milk. Season to taste with garlic salt. Continue to simmer gently for 20 minutes, or until the chicken is tender and the sauce has thickened.

Serve hot with rice and tomatoes.

Pork with Eggplant

Pork and eggplant might seem strange bedfellows, but in West Africa we regularly combine the two in cooking. Adding apples makes the dish a hybrid, and creates an even more unusual flavor. Served with rice, mashed yams, or potatoes, this makes a delicious meal. It's when you blend ingredients together in exotic ways that you know you are "eating with many tongues."

SERVES 4

1/2 cup peanut oil

4 to 6 lean pork cutlets

4 tablespoons flour mixed with 1 teaspoon salt

3 tablespoons cold water

Spices of choice

1 teaspoon hot paprika

4 medium eggplants, or 8 to 10 garden eggs (small, white tropical eggplants), peeled and diced

2 tart apples, diced (optional)

Heat the oil in a large, heavy-based pan. Coat the pork with the flour and salt mixture, and sauté in the oil until golden. Add the water, spices, and paprika, and simmer on low heat until the meat is tender. Stir in the eggplants and apples, and cook for about 20 minutes, or until everything is cooked and the sauce has thickened.

Serve hot.

Creole

A unique combination of French, Spanish, and African heritages have evolved into the culture of Creole. A term originally used in Latin America, *Creole* distinguished the descendants of the European colonialists from the Amerindians, Africans, and later immigrants. Over time these groups have mixed, and today Creole has formed a unique part of the culture, particularly in Martinique, Guadeloupe, and Louisiana. The resultant cuisine is a celebrated blend of African vegetable and fish ingredients; the clever use of spices and herbs, so much a style of Spain; and the refined sauces of France. While the strong African signature remains, the roux and piquant sauces of French and Spanish Creoles have replaced the heavy emphasis on onions, ginger, and large quantities of chiles, which are integral to African cooking.

Of Flowers and Beautiful Waters

Some of the original Amerindian inhabitants of the Caribbean, the Caribs, called Martinique the "island of flowers." Its sister island Guadeloupe, lying 199 miles north, was called Karukera or "the island of beautiful waters" by its original Arawak Indians. Guadeloupe's name was changed when Christopher Columbus charted it in 1493 and called it Santa Maria de Guadeloupe de Estra-maduros.

Guadeloupe is actually comprised of two small islands, Grande-Terre to the east and Bass-Terre to the west, separated by a sea channel called the Rivière Salée.

Martinique and Guadeloupe form the westernmost boundary of French territory, because both are possessions of France.

Mangoes in Citrus Syrup

The mango, Mangifera indica, *is an incredibly versatile fruit. On some Caribbean islands, it is used in mango pie, mango drinks, mango mousse, and mango chutney. The leaves of the mango tree produce a yellow dye, and on some islands the leaves are used as cattle fodder. Mango tree bark yields a tanin, and the wood is used in ship building. This dessert is one of the easiest, and most delicious, uses of mangoes.*

SERVES 4

¼ cup freshly squeezed lime juice

5 cups water

4 cups superfine sugar

1 tablespoon finely grated lime zest

1 tablespoon finely grated lemon zest

4 fresh lime leaves, cleaned, dried, and very finely sliced, plus 4 fresh lime leaves, cleaned and dried, for garnish

4 large mangoes, chilled if desired

In a medium heavy-based pan, combine the lime juice, water, sugar, citrus zests, and lime leaves. Stir over medium-low heat until the sugar dissolves and the mixture boils. Decrease the heat and allow the mixture to simmer uncovered for 10 to 15 minutes, or until the syrup thickens slightly.

Using a sharp knife, cut through each mango lengthwise on either side of the central seed to give you 2 mango cheeks. Carefully peel away the skins so the mango cheeks retain their domed shapes. Attractively arrange the mango cheeks in a serving dish, and drizzle the warm syrup over the tops.

Serve hot or cold, with each serving garnished with a fresh lime leaf or a thin spiral of either lemon or lime zest.

JAMAICA

OFFICIAL TITLE: Jamaica

CAPITAL CITY: Kingston

OFFICIAL LANGUAGE: English, although Creole and Patois are widely spoken

CURRENCY: Jamaican dollar (J$) = 100 cents

CASH CROPS FOR EXPORT: Sugar, cocoa, coffee, citrus fruits, bananas, pimentoes and ginger

FOOD CROPS: Rice, yams, bananas and other fruits, vegetables, livestock, and fish

TOTAL LAND AREA: 4,247 square miles

Plantain Chips

Where would we be without this ever-versatile fruit? As far as I'm concerned, you can never have too many plantain recipes. Plantain preparations have a mass appeal; everybody loves them: kids, adults, young, old, and even pets! Be sure that you use unripe plantains, which are green.

SERVES 4 TO 6

4 unripe plantains

1 teaspoon vegetable oil

Juice of 1 fresh lime

Salt

Freshly ground black pepper (optional)

Vegetable oil, for deep-frying

Salted peanuts, as accompaniment (optional)

Preheat the oven to 250°F/140°C.

Plantain skin is thicker than that of sweet bananas and its skin tends to cling to the flesh underneath. But there is an easy way of tackling the task of peeling plantains. Trim off the ends of the plantain, then cut it in half. Make 4 vertical slits at even intervals into each half of the trimmed plantain. Make sure the slits are deep enough to reach the flesh beneath.

Oil your hands lightly with the vegetable oil to prevent dark staining of the skin by the sap. Starting with 1 slit at a time, from the narrower end, pull the skin away from the flesh beneath. Peel off any remaining stubborn skin with a sharp knife.

Rub the flesh with lime juice, then cut very thin slices, making them round or cutting on the diagonal for ovals. Season with salt and pepper. Drain any excess liquid.

Heat vegetable oil for frying in a deep skillet, and fry the plantain chips in small batches for 3 to 5 minutes, or until crisp and golden brown. Using a slotted spoon, remove from the oil and drain on paper towels. Keep warm in the oven until all the chips are cooked.

Serve immediately with peanuts.

Stuffed Papaya

Although papaya is treated as a fruit in Western countries, its versatility is exploited more in Africa and the West Indies. Like Africans, Jamaicans use unripe, green baby papayas as a substitute in the absence of eggplants and other vegetables. In its soft, ripe, orange form, it is used the world over as a fruit or in puddings of various kinds. Papaya is another of the extremely beneficial fruits and vegetables that have both medicinal and culinary properties.

SERVES 4

¼ cup vegetable oil

2 green onions, diced

3 cloves garlic, diced

2 fresh red chiles, diced (optional)

1 pound (500 g) lean ground beef

2 teaspoons tomato paste mixed with 2 teaspoons cold water

2 tomatoes, blanched, peeled, and diced

Salt

Freshly ground black pepper

2 large, unripe papayas, peeled, seeded, and halved

2 cups boiling water

¾ cup grated Parmesan cheese

4 tomatoes

Minced fresh chives, for garnish

Preheat the oven to 400°F/200°C. Heat the oil in a large pan and sauté the onions, garlic, and chiles for 5 to 7 minutes, or until the onions are golden. Stir in the beef and cook for 10 minutes. Add the tomato paste mixture and the tomatoes to the pan. Season with salt and pepper. Cook on low heat for 10 to 15 minutes, or until the mixture thickens slightly. Remove from the heat and set aside.

In a large dish, cover the papaya halves with the water and let stand for 10 to 15 minutes. Remove the papaya and dry with paper towels. Lightly grease a large baking dish and arrange the papaya halves in it side by side. Fill each half with the beef mixture, and top with the Parmesan cheese.

Arrange the whole tomatoes around the papaya halves, and bake for 30 to 45 minutes, or until the papaya is soft and cooked.

Serve hot, topped with chives and black pepper.

Jamaican Patties

This recipe is a Jamaican favorite and is particularly popular among the Rastafarian community because it fits into their ital *food philosophy. Ital means food should be as close as possible to its natural state without preservatives or additives. These patties are tasty and nutritious, especially when served with chutney, relish, or tomato sauce—I'm hooked!*

MAKES 24 PATTIES

FILLING

2¹/₂ cups lima beans

1 cup corn oil

1 large yellow onion, minced

4 large cloves garlic, minced

2 large carrots, peeled and minced

1 large red bell pepper, seeded and minced

2 Scotch bonnet or fresh red chiles, seeded and minced

³/₄ pound (375 g) button mushrooms, cleaned and minced

2 large sweet potatoes, peeled and diced

¹/₂ cup uncooked corn kernels

Salt

Freshly ground black pepper

2 cups whole-wheat bread crumbs

PASTRY

¹/₂ cup all-purpose flour

¹ cup self-rising flour

2 cups whole-wheat flour

2¹/₂ teaspoons ground turmeric

1 teaspoon salt

1¹/₂ cups vegetable shortening, chilled and diced

Chilled water, as needed

Place the lima beans in a large pan. Add water to cover by 2 inches. Bring to a boil, decrease the heat, and simmer, covered, for 30 to 50 minutes, or until the beans are tender. Drain, reserving 2 cups of the cooking water.

While the beans are cooking, make the pastry. Sift together the flours, turmeric, and salt into a bowl. Rub in the vegetable shortening with your fingers until the mixture resembles coarse bread crumbs.

Using a blunt, stainless-steel knife or a flat spoon, mix in enough chilled water to gather the mixture into a soft, pliable dough. Do not overhandle the pastry. Shape it quickly into a ball. Cover the bowl with a damp dish towel or cheesecloth, or put the pastry in a clean plastic bag and leave it in a cool place or the refrigerator for 30 minutes.

To make the filling, heat the corn oil in a large, heavy-based pan on medium heat. Fry the onion and garlic for about 5 minutes, or until they are soft and golden. Add the carrots, bell pepper, chiles, and mushrooms and continue frying gently for 10 to 15 minutes, or until all the vegetables have softened and are half cooked.

Add the lima beans, the 2 cups reserved cooking water, the potatoes, and the sweet corn. Season with salt and pepper, cover the pan, decrease the heat, and simmer on low for 20 minutes, or until the potatoes and corn kernels are tender. Remove from the heat, stir in the bread crumbs, and set aside to cool.

Preheat the oven to 375°F/190°C. To make the patties, divide the chilled pastry into small, manageable portions for rolling out. On a lightly floured board or working surface, roll out each portion to a thickness of 1/4 inch. Using a medium-size cookie cutter or saucer, cut out 24 rounds.

Place 1 to 2 teaspoons of the cooled filling on the center of each round, and moisten the edge of each round with a little chilled water. Carefully fold over half of each pastry round to form a crescent-shaped patty. Crimp the edge with the prongs of a fork to make a decorative seal. Repeat this process until you've used all the pastry and filling.

Lightly grease and flour a baking sheet and carefully arrange the patties about 1 inch apart on the sheet. Bake in the oven for 25 to 30 minutes, or until golden brown.

Serve hot or cold.

Akee and Saltfish

This well-known Jamaican dish reminds me of a Ghanaian favorite called koobi ne kosua froye, *which my mother used to make for me. So popular is akee and saltfish in Jamaica, it has reached the status of national dish, and songs have been written about akee.*

Akee is the edible yellow fruit found in the seedpods of a tropical West African tree, Blighia sapida, *that now grows in Jamaica. It is difficult to obtain fresh akee outside Africa and Jamaica (it is sometimes available in Florida and Hawaii), but you can find canned akee. Fresh akee should not be eaten unless it comes from a fully opened seedpod and has been cooked. This is memorialized in a Jamaican riddle:*

> *Riddle me this, riddle me that:*
> *My daddy sent me out to get me a wife,*
> *But he warned, "Only pick the smiling ones.*
> *If they don't smile they'll kill you."*
> *Answer: The akee*

SERVES 4

1 pound (500 g) dried salted fish

3 tablespoons vegetable oil

2 yellow onions, diced

¼-pound (125 g) piece smoked ham hock or bacon, diced

2 red or green bell peppers, seeded and diced

3 tomatoes, diced

1 tablespoon finely chopped fresh basil, or pinch of dried oregano

Salt

Freshly ground black pepper

1 15-ounce (470-g) can akee, drained

Vegetables and herbs (such as tomatoes, onion, parsley, or cilantro), diced, for garnish

Soak the salted fish in water to cover overnight to remove excess salt. Rinse in cold water. Bone, skin, and flake the fish into small pieces.

In a large skillet, heat the oil and sauté the onions for about 3 minutes. Add the smoked hock, peppers, tomatoes, and basil. Season with salt and pepper.

Gently cook for 3 to 5 minutes, stirring regularly. Add the flaked fish and cook for 5 to 10 minutes. Stir in the drained akee, mix well, and cook on low heat for 10 minutes, stirring gently but regularly to prevent burning.

Serve hot with the garnish of your choice.

Chicken with Rum and Coconut

It would be criminal to write about my favorite Jamaican recipes and not include this popular one that uses the rum that Jamaica produces to perfection. This dish is very rich and designed to impress. Serve it with boiled rice tossed with mixed herbs and fresh steamed vegetables of your choice.

SERVES 4

12 chicken wings or small drumsticks

4 tablespoons butter

6 tablespoons vegetable oil

4 to 6 tablespoons Jamaican rum

2 or 3 chicken bouillon cubes, crushed

Garlic powder, for seasoning

Freshly ground black pepper

1²/₃ cups coconut cream

1¹/₄ cups heavy cream

¹/₂ pound small button mushrooms, cleaned

Rinse the chicken wings and cut off and discard the little jointed fingerlike tips. Cut each wing in half to produce a flat part and a fleshy minidrumstick.

In a large, heavy-based pan, heat the butter and oil. Sauté the chicken wings until golden and cooked. You may have to fry in small batches. When all the chicken wings are cooked, return them to the pan on the stove and decrease the heat. This next part is tricky, so be careful. Quickly pour the rum over the chicken wings, and light a match to set the rum alight. Carefully tilt the pan to ensure all the chicken wings are flambéed.

When the flames die down, add the bouillon cubes, garlic powder, lots of pepper, the coconut cream, and the cream. Stir well to mix and simmer gently for 15 to 20 minutes. Add the mushrooms and simmer on low to medium heat until the sauce thickens.

Serve hot.

The Language Connection

Jamaica's earliest settlers were the Arawak Indians, and the name of the island today derives from the Arawak word *Xaymaca,* which means "island of the springs." It is commonplace to describe the Amerindians of the Caribbean as the "peaceful" Arawaks and the "warlike" Caribs, but whatever their dispositions, neither group lasted long after European colonization began.

What has remained as a constant reminder of these people is fragments of their languages, still in use today. Besides the island names of Jamaica, Cuba and Martinique, words such as tobacco, hammock, canoe, hurricane, iguana, maize, and potato have endured.

Also enduring in the language of many Caribbean islands are examples of languages carried by slaves from several different African countries. Many have been modified over time, to be sure, but there are innumerable examples of words from different African languages, such as Yoruba and Ashanti, that still exist in the melting pot of Jamaica.

Examples include *fufu,* the name of a dumpling popular both in West African and West Indian countries (it is sometimes spelled *foofoo*); *abé,* the edible seed of the palmnut; akee, the favorite breakfast fruit of Jamaica, which originally came from West Africa; *abeng,* a style of wind instrument made from a bull's horn; the *kumina,* an adaptation of an Ashanti ancestral possession cult, that in Ghana is called *akom-ina;* and *patu, the word for an* owl.

Personal names also continue to form a link between the language of the African heritage and the Jamaicans of today. Recorded in history are the names of Maroon generals and chiefs, such as Cudjoe, Quao, Nana Acheampong, and Taky, which are names still in use in Ghana. Another example is the name Quashie, which in Africa is Kwesi (pronounced quarshie); the spelling and pronunciation might have evolved over time and distance, but the African heritage remains.

Jerk Pork

There is no specific English meaning for the word jerk *in this Jamaican specialty. Jerking is said to be a secret Arawak Indian method of cooking pig.*

However, jerk pork is, tongue-in-cheek, pork with a kick: grilled pork with seasoning that makes it sit up and be noticed, like the Ghanaian pork called domedo. *I believe the modern Jamaican jerk pork evolved from original Arawak Indian and African versions. This recipe is a modified combination of jerk pork and* domedo.

Jerk Pork is so delicious that the anticipation of eating it is enough to make me click my fingers and shake my head with excitement. The marinade recipe below can be used for meat, fish, chicken, seafood, or vegetables. I find it especially delicious on chicken; see the Note that follows for chicken directions. Serve jerk pork with rice and peas for an authentic Jamaican meal.

SERVES 4 TO 6

3 pounds (1.5 kg) pork cutlets

2 fresh limes or lemons, cut into quarters

Crisp, fresh green salad with wedges of fresh lime, as accompaniment

Rice and Peas, Guadeloupe Style (page 177), as accompaniment

2 teaspoons freshly ground white pepper

1 tablespoon light brown sugar

6 tablespoons extra-virgin olive oil

JERK MARINADE

1 large yellow onion, coarsely chopped

3 green onions, minced

3 tablespoons soy sauce

1 tablespoon fresh thyme

1 tablespoon hot paprika

1 teaspoon ground allspice

1 or 2 Scotch bonnet chiles, seeded and minced

2 tablespoons white wine vinegar

Rub the pork cutlets with 1¹/₂ limes, and slash them in several places so the marinade can penetrate to the core of the meat.

Combine all the ingredients for the jerk marinade in a food processor, and pulse intermittently to break the ingredients into pulp without blending them too smoothly. It is good for the marinade to have some texture. Transfer the marinade to a large bowl.

Using clean hands, toss the pork cutlets in the marinade, coating thoroughly. Cover and set aside in the refrigerator overnight.

Preheat the oven to 350°F/180°C, or fire up your barbecue.

If you are cooking in the oven, coat a roasting pan or baking dish with a little olive oil and place the marinated pork in it. Spoon some marinade over the meat, and reserve the remaining marinade. Bake for 40 to 45 minutes, or until cooked through. Turn regularly to ensure even cooking.

If you are cooking on a barbecue, arrange the meat evenly on the grill rack. Grill for 4 to 5 minutes on each side, or until just faintly pink inside.

Put the leftover marinade in a small saucepan. Add a squeeze of fresh lime juice from the remaining $1/2$ lime. Place on low heat and cook, stirring continuously, for 5 to 7 minutes.

Cut the jerk pork into thick slices and arrange on a serving platter. Douse with the cooked marinade from both the baking dish, if used, and the saucepan. Arrange salad and lime wedges around the meat, and serve immediately.

NOTE: This recipe is also delicious made with chicken. For chicken, use 8 bone-in, skin-on chicken pieces. Proceed as directed for pork. If you decide to grill the chicken, arrange skin side down on the grill, cover the grill, and cook for 8 to 10 minutes. Turn the chicken and cook for 10 to 15 minutes longer, or until the meat is opaque throughout and pulls away from the bone.

Sweet Potato Pone

You can make pone from cornmeal, sweet potatoes, yams, or gari, but my favorite recipe uses sweet potatoes. It can be eaten hot or cold, but I love it cold because the flavor of the ginger seems stronger. Serve pone as a dessert with cream, as an accompaniment to roast pork or poultry, or alone, hot or cold, as a snack.

SERVES 4 TO 6

4 sweet potatoes or yams, peeled and grated

3 cups grated pumpkin

1 tablespoon peeled and grated fresh ginger

4 tablespoons butter, melted

1/2 cup flaked, dried coconut or freshly grated coconut

1 cup cold water

1 1/4 cups superfine sugar

1 teaspoon vanilla extract

1 teaspoon freshly grated nutmeg

4 tablespoons golden raisins (optional)

4 tablespoons dark raisins (optional)

Preheat the oven to 350°F/180°C.

In a large mixing bowl, combine all the ingredients and mix well. Grease 2 9-inch pie dishes and pour in the mixture. Smooth the tops. Bake for 1 hour, or until firm.

Serve hot or cold.

Cornmeal Pudding

Cornmeal, like black-eyed peas, is a traditional part of soul food, whether it is found in the West Indies, Latin America, African-America, or Africa itself. With the addition of coconut and sugar (from sugarcane), the humble original cornmeal has taken on a sweet Jamaican identity that has become a delicious tradition in virtually every Jamaican home.

SERVES 4

1 small coconut, or 1 cup coconut cream mixed with 2¾ cups cold water

3 cups yellow cornmeal or polenta

⅔ to 1¼ cups sugar, to taste

4 tablespoons butter, melted

Salt and freshly grated nutmeg, vanilla extract, ground cinnamon, or ground allspice, for seasoning

Preheat the oven to 400°F/200°C. Grate the coconut and squeeze out 3¾ cups coconut milk, or combine the coconut cream with the water. Place in a bowl and mix in the cornmeal, sugar, and butter. Season with salt and a spice or vanilla. Pour the mixture into an 8-inch buttered baking dish.

Bake for 1 hour, or until firm but still a bit moist. Remove from the oven, let cool a little, and serve.

Avocado Ice Cream

I know that most people think of avocados as something to add to salads or soups or as a part of a main course, but this recipe is proof that they can be made into an unusual and delicious dessert—ice cream, in fact!

SERVES 4

2 avocados

1 teaspoon freshly squeezed
    lemon juice

4 tablespoons superfine sugar

BASIC EGG CUSTARD

3 eggs

1/3 cup superfine sugar

2 cups milk

1 teaspoon vanilla extract

Peel and pit the avocados, and mash the flesh with the lemon juice and sugar.

To make the basic egg custard, lightly beat the eggs and sugar together. In a small pan, bring the milk almost to a boil, but do not boil. Add the vanilla extract, and quickly stir the milk mixture into the egg and sugar mixture. Cook the custard in the top half of a double boiler over hot water. Stir continuously until the mixture thickens and coats the back of a spoon. Remove from the heat and let cool.

When cool, combine the avocado mix with the custard. Stir well, then chill in the freezer for 3 to 4 hours. Remove, beat well to make it smoother, and chill for a second time until firm.

Serve cold.

NOTE: In traditional African homes, electric ice cream makers are as rare as hen's teeth. But should you own one of these labor-saving machines and prefer to freeze your ice cream in it, by all means do so. Simply put the egg-avocado custard in your ice cream maker, and then follow the manufacturer's instructions for freezing.

Christmastime Mango Mousse

I love mangoes and I love this dessert! It's colorful and easy to prepare, and the payback in taste is simply sensational. But it is fattening because of the cream content, which is why I call it a Christmastime mousse. That way it gets treated with the utmost respect and is eaten on special occasions only. Besides, mangoes are at their most abundant in most tropical countries around Christmas, and this is an exotic variation of the regular fruit desserts.

SERVES 4 TO 6

3 to 4 large, ripe mangoes

1/3 cup superfine sugar

1/4 cup mango liqueur or other flavored liqueur, such as Grand Marnier or Triple Sec

2 cups heavy cream

Mint sprigs, for garnish

Strawberries, thinly sliced, for garnish (optional)

Wash the mangoes, dry with paper towels, and cut them open with a sharp knife. Scoop out all the flesh into a bowl. Process the pulp to a smooth purée in a blender or food processor; do not use a juicer.

Push the mango pulp through a fine-mesh sieve to rid it of any fibers and to keep the pulp smooth. Cover and set aside.

Combine the sugar and liqueur in a cup, and stir together until the sugar mostly dissolves. Add to the mango pulp.

Start whipping the cream, and slowly add the mango pulp as you whip. Continue whipping until the mango and cream are well combined and the mixture is thick, smooth, and creamy. Pour into parfait or other dessert glasses. Chill in the refrigerator, not the freezer, until ready to serve. Garnish with sprigs of mint and strawberries before serving.

CUBA

OFFICIAL TITLE: Republic of Cuba

CAPITAL CITY: Havana (Habana)

OFFICIAL LANGUAGE: Spanish, although English is used in business

CURRENCY: Cuban peso = 100 centavos

CASH CROPS FOR EXPORT: Sugar, cotton, tobacco, and fish

FOOD CROPS: Rice, corn, cotton, cassava, sweet potatoes, potatoes, other vegetables, fruit, livestock, and fish

TOTAL LAND AREA: 44,209 square miles

Fried Plantains

Though part of the same family as bananas, plantains, Musa sapientum, *cannot be eaten raw by humans; they need to be cooked first. Plantains are bigger, starchier, less sweet, and more versatile than bananas, and they're regarded as vegetables. Along with beans, cassava, onions, tomatoes, and sweet potatoes, plantains have traveled widely among the black communities of the world. There is a myriad of recipes for plantains, but this is one of the simplest. Be sure to use ripe plantains, which are yellow, not green, unripe plantains.*

SERVES 4

3 or 4 whole ripe plantains
Salt
Freshly ground black pepper
Vegetable oil, for deep-frying

Trim off both ends of each plantain with a knife. Score firmly, but not too deeply, vertically from one end of the plantain to the other. Remove the skin.

There are many styles of cutting plantains, from the fancy to the plain, depending on whom you want to please—yourself or others. I suggest that you start with a simple style and evolve your own later.

Lay the peeled plantain on a cutting board, holding it firmly at one end. Starting from just above the farthest end, cut off thick portions diagonally. Each plantain should yield about 6 pieces. Sprinkle with salt and pepper and toss the plantain portions together. It is better to make the portions thicker to start with, because they are easier to turn while cooking.

Heat the vegetable oil in a deep fryer or very deep pot. When it is very hot but not boiling, gently fry the plantain portions until they are golden brown on both sides. Lift out, drain, set aside, and keep hot. Serve with the dish of your choice. With roasted peanuts, this becomes a wonderful snack.

NOTE: As a variation, peel 2 or 3 ripe plantains in the same way, and cut them into thick, 1-inch vertical strips, into cubes, or into rounds. Season with a blended mixture of 2 fresh red chiles, 1 small piece of fresh ginger, peeled and grated, pinch of salt, and 1/2 cup water. Drain and deep-fry.

This variation is also very popular in West Africa, where it is called *kéléwélé* and is sold on street corners at night.

Red Sauce

This aromatic and piquant sauce is especially popular eaten with black-eyed peas, which can be very dry. It is also excellent served with plantains or boiled rice.

MAKES 4 CUPS

1 cup olive oil

3 tomatoes, blanched, peeled, and diced

3 to 4 cloves garlic, diced

1 teaspoon sugar

1 teaspoon cayenne pepper

1 teaspoon minced fresh basil

2 teaspoons dried oregano

Freshly ground black pepper

6 tablespoons malt vinegar

In a small pan, heat the oil and sauté the tomatoes for 5 to 10 minutes, or until they are soft. Stir in the garlic, sugar, cayenne pepper, basil, and oregano, and season with black pepper. Simmer on low heat, stirring regularly, for 20 to 30 minutes, or until the sauce thickens. Remove from the heat, let stand for 3 to 5 minutes, and stir in the vinegar.

Let cool and set aside. Cover and store in the refrigerator for up to 1 week.

Moors and Christians

The name of this dish comes from the color mix of the dark beans and white rice. Moors are Muslims of mixed Berber and Arab descent, many of whom live in Morocco in northwest Africa. While this is another dish originating in Africa (where it is sometimes called waatsé—pronounced wah-chay), it has traveled west with the African people. In Cuba it is served with fried plantains (page 202), just as it is in West Africa.

SERVES 4

6 cups dried black-eyed peas,
　soaked in water overnight

4 cups water

2 teaspoons salt

1 large yellow onion, diced

2 cloves garlic, diced

6 tablespoons olive oil

1 cup long-grain white rice

Salt

Freshly ground black pepper

Fried Plantains (page 202),
　as accompaniment

Drain the peas and rinse in cold water. Pour the water into a large saucepan and add the salt. Bring to a boil and par-boil the peas for 20 to 30 minutes, or until they are about half cooked; they should not be soft. Remove from the heat and drain off the water, saving both the bean water and the beans.

In a large pot, sauté the onion and garlic in the olive oil until they begin to brown. Add the rice and $2\frac{1}{8}$ cups of the reserved bean water. If there is more left, reserve it for later. Stir well, season with salt and pepper, and simmer for 10 to 15 minutes on low heat.

Stir in the parboiled beans and add the remaining bean water (if any) or more water seasoned with a little salt if the rice is too dry. Cook slowly on very low heat, checking frequently for water content. The dish is done when the beans and rice are both tender.

Serve hot, topped with the plantains.

Creole Casserole

This recipe is like a little beacon linking the African continent to Cuba. It has long been a clever and delicious way to use up unattractive cuts of meat or poultry or to recycle leftovers; I suspect that during the era of slavery, poor cuts of meat were the only ones available to blacks. This recipe, however, has traveled through generations of black Cuban families and has been much improved along the way. A filling dish, it makes an excellent winter soup and is best served with warm bread, boiled white rice, or alone.

SERVES 4 TO 6

3/4 cup dried red kidney beans, soaked in water overnight

2/3 cup vegetable oil

1/2 pound (250 g) pig's feet, or 1 cup giblets, or 4 pieces chicken, cut into 2-inch chunks

2 yellow onions, diced

4 cloves garlic, diced

4 small fresh red chiles

4 large tomatoes, blanched, peeled, and diced

2 teaspoons dried oregano

1 teaspoon mushroom or soy sauce

8 1/2 cups cold water

2 bay leaves

1 teaspoon salt

1 potato, peeled and diced

1 sweet potato, peeled and diced

1 yam, peeled and diced

1 1/2 cups peeled and diced pumpkin

1 ripe plantain or banana, peeled, ends trimmed, and cut into 6 rounds

Salt

Freshly ground black pepper

4 to 5 tablespoons cornstarch blended with 2/3 cup cold water

Drain the beans and rinse in cold water. In a large pot, combine the kidney beans with water to cover by 2 inches. Bring to a boil, then decrease the heat and simmer, covered, for 20 minutes. Drain and set aside.

In a large pot, heat the oil and sauté the pig's feet with the onions, garlic, chiles, tomatoes, oregano, and mushroom sauce for about 10 minutes. Add the water, bay leaves, and salt. Cook over low to medium heat for 10 minutes, or until the meat is soft and tender.

Add the kidney beans to the meat and cook for 10 to 15 minutes. Then, at 10-minute intervals, add the potato, then the sweet potato, the yam, the pumpkin, and finally the plantain. Simmer on low heat for 10 minutes. Season with salt and pepper, and then mix in the cornstarch mixture. Simmer for 20 to 30 minutes. Remove from the heat and skim off the excess oil.

Serve hot.

NOTE: During cooking, try not to stir the dish too much. Less stirring makes for more attractive and recognizable vegetables in the finished casserole.

Black-Eyed Peas with Fish

FRIJOLES NEGROS CON PESCADO

The ever-popular and useful black-eyed peas pop up in recipes in Cuba, too. This time, the beans are combined with smoked or fried fish—with a Spanish touch. Serve this dish with grilled or fried plantains (page 202) and boiled arroz blanco *(white rice).*

SERVES 4 TO 6

4 cups dried black-eyed peas, soaked in water overnight

Salt

1/2 cup vegetable oil

3 large yellow onions, diced

3 tomatoes, blanched, peeled, and diced

2 teaspoons ground turmeric

2 to 3 fresh red chiles, diced (optional)

1/2 pound smoked or fried fish, boned, skinned, and cut into small chunks

1/2 cup dried shrimp

Drain the peas and rinse with fresh water several times. Place in a pan with water to cover generously and add salt. Bring to a boil and cook for 30 to 40 minutes, or until the beans are soft but not mushy. Drain and set aside.

In another large pan, heat the oil and fry the onions until golden. Add the tomatoes, turmeric, and chiles and stir well to prevent burning. Cook for 3 minutes on medium heat, stirring continuously. Add the fish and shrimp and stir. Decrease the heat and cook for 3 more minutes. Stir in the cooked beans and simmer for 10 to 15 minutes, or until the fish is tender and cooked.

Serve hot.

Rice *and* Fish in Rum

I had to have this versatile and delicious recipe translated because it was in Spanish. Given to me by Mrs. Emilia Marchante of Cuba, it is versatile because you can vary the taste to suit yourself by adding different spices. I love it because it contains rice and rum!

SERVES 4

FISH STOCK

2 pounds (1 kg) fish heads and bones

5 cups water

1 bay leaf

1 small red bell pepper, diced

1 large white onion, diced

1 tomato, diced

Salt

RICE AND FISH IN RUM

1/2 teaspoon dried oregano or ground cumin

1 teaspoon freshly ground black pepper

1 tablespoon ground cinnamon

6 tablespoons freshly squeezed lemon juice or malt vinegar

Salt

1 pound (500 g) firm, white-fleshed fish, boned and cut into big chunks

2 cups long-grain white or brown rice

4 1/4 cups fish stock (see recipe above)

1/2 cup vegetable oil

1 onion, diced

3 cloves garlic, diced

2 tablespoons soy sauce or Worcestershire sauce

1/2 cup dark rum

1 teaspoon saffron powder or ground turmeric

To make the fish stock, in a large pot, simmer the ingredients, covered, for about 1 hour on medium to low heat. Remove from the heat, strain through a fine-mesh sieve, and discard the solids.

To make the rice and fish in rum, combine the oregano, pepper, cinnamon, and lemon juice, and season with salt. Marinate the fish in this mixture, covered, in the refrigerator for 2 to 4 hours. Soak the rice in 2 1/8 cups of the fish stock.

Heat the oil in a large pan and sauté the onion and garlic for 3 to 5 minutes, or until they start to brown. Quickly add the soy sauce and the fish and its marinade. Cook for 2 to 3 minutes. Add the rum, the remaining fish stock, and the saffron. Adjust the seasoning to taste, and add the steeped rice.

Stir together well, taking care not to break up the fish too much. Cook on very low heat for about 45 minutes, or until the rice is cooked. You may need to add more water during the cooking process, depending on whether you use white or brown rice.

Serve hot with fresh vegetables of your choice.

Cuba

Discovering Cuba during his first voyage to the region in 1492, Christopher Columbus at first thought he had reached China. This did not deter him from naming the island Juana in honor of the daughter of his patrons, Ferdinand and Isabella of Spain. The name was later changed to Santiago, favored in many areas of Spanish colonization to honor their country's patron saint, but it eventually reverted to Cuba, the name used by the island's original Arawak Indian inhabitants.

Cuba was colonized early, in 1511, and the Arawaks were enslaved and virtually died out in a few years. They were replaced, as so often happened in the history of the Caribbean islands, by slaves from West Africa. Despite this, unlike many of the other islands, the majority of Cuba's population is still dominated by those of European descent.

Sweet Potato Cake

There are different types of sweet potatoes, which range from the purple-skinned variety (the sweetest) to the orange-skinned and white-skinned varieties, depending on where they grow in the tropics. I like to top this cake with whipped cream or served it with custard.

SERVES 4

1/4 cup ginger wine or rum mixed with 1/2 cup water

1/2 teaspoon vanilla extract

1 1/4 cups sugar

1 pound (500 g) sweet potatoes, peeled, boiled, and mashed

1/2 cup butter, melted

3 eggs

1/2 cup flour

2 teaspoons baking powder

1 teaspoon salt

Preheat the oven to 350°F/180°C.

In a large mixing bowl, combine the ginger wine, vanilla, and sugar. Mix in the sweet potatoes with the butter. Separate the egg yolks from the whites (set the whites aside), beat the yolks well, and add to the sweet potato mixture.

Sift together the flour, baking powder, and salt and fold into the sweet potato mixture. Beat the egg whites until they form soft peaks. Fold into the sweet potato mixture. Lightly grease a 10-inch springform pan, and pour the mixture into it.

Bake for 45 minutes to 1 hour. Check with a skewer after 40 minutes. If the skewer comes out clean, the cake is cooked. Remove from the oven, let stand for 10 to 15 minutes, and then turn out onto a wire rack.

Slice and serve.

LOUISIANA

STATUS: A southern state of the United States of America
CAPITAL CITY: Baton Rouge
OFFICIAL LANGUAGE: English
CURRENCY: Dollar (US$) = 100 cents
FOOD CROPS: Corn, soybeans, and wheat
TOTAL LAND AREA: 48,649 square miles

Gumbo

With the increasing popularity of Cajun and Creole cuisine the world over, gumbo hardly needs an introduction. A thick soup made from okra, crab, spicy sausage, chicken, and spices, and laden with boiled rice, it looks like a watery risotto. It is usually served in a deep soup dish rather than a bowl, and you will get maximum pleasure from eating it with a spoon and your fingers.

SERVES 4 TO 6

¹/₂ cup butter

4 tablespoons cornstarch

1 small yellow onion, diced

3 cloves garlic, crushed

1 small green bell pepper, seeded and diced

4 stalks celery, chopped

1 pound (500 g) okra, topped, tailed, and sliced

4 tomatoes, blanched, peeled, and diced

1 pound (500 g) shrimp, peeled and deveined

4 small crayfish or crab claws

4 roasted or fried chicken wings, halved

1 teaspoon dried oregano or marjoram

1 or 2 bay leaves

4¹/₄ cups hot water mixed with 2 crushed chicken bouillon cubes

¹/₂ pound (250 g) smoked ham or spicy pork sausage, diced

1 teaspoon freshly grated nutmeg

Salt

Freshly ground black pepper

1 to 2 tablespoons gumbo filé powder (see Note)

8 cups boiled long-grain white rice

In a large pan, melt the butter and blend in the cornstarch. Stir well on medium heat for 5 minutes, or until light brown. Add the onion, garlic, bell pepper, celery, and okra, and fry for 10 minutes. Add the tomatoes and shrimp and cook on low heat for 5 to 10 minutes, taking care not to burn. Add the crayfish, chicken, oregano, bay leaves, and bouillon water. Cook for about 20 minutes. Add the smoked ham and nutmeg and stir well. Season with salt and pepper, cover, and simmer for 20 minutes.

Decrease the heat to very low and, in a small bowl, mix the gumbo filé into a smooth, runny paste with an equal amount of warm water and a small portion of strained sauce from the cooking pan. Add the gumbo filé paste to the sauce. Simmer very gently, stirring continuously, for 3 to 5 minutes.

To serve, scoop boiled rice into the bottom of a big bowl. Arrange the chicken, crab, ham, and shrimp with a generous portion of the gumbo sauce on top. Serve hot.

NOTE: Gumbo is the original West African word for okra, but gumbo filé is the secret ingredient in a delicious gumbo. It is made from powdered sassafras leaves, and it thickens the gumbo sauce. Once added, stir on very low heat for 3 to 5 minutes.

Vegetable-Herb Bake

Folks from Louisiana waste nothing if they can help it, so all leftovers are recycled into even more delicious recipes. This all-vegetable recipe goes well with the King of Gumbos served on Good Fridays in southern Louisiana. The King of Gumbos adds fresh green vegetables to the traditional gumbo recipe (opposite). This is delicious paired with a fresh, crisp, green salad and some Garlic Sauce (page 80) or with Gumbo (opposite).

SERVES 4

3 eggs

1/4 bunch spinach, very finely shredded

1 large carrot, peeled and grated

1 small red bell pepper, seeded and diced

6 tablespoons minced fresh chives

1 tablespoon minced fresh basil

1 tablespoon minced fresh dill

4 tablespoons self-rising flour

1 teaspoon salt

1 teaspoon freshly ground black pepper

3/4 cup grated Cheddar or Gouda cheese

1 tablespoon minced fresh cilantro

1 tablespoon chopped fresh flat-leaf parsley,

Preheat the oven to 375°F/190°C.

Separate the egg whites from the yolks, and set the whites aside. Combine the egg yolks and the spinach, carrot, bell pepper, chives, basil, dill, flour, salt, and pepper in a large bowl. Mix well. Whisk the egg whites in a separate bowl until stiff peaks form. Using a wooden spoon, stir 2 spoonfuls of egg whites into the vegetable mixture, then fold the remaining whisked egg whites into the mixture, taking care to work from the sides of the bowl toward the center to maintain the lightness of the mixture.

Grease a large bundt pan and carefully pour the mixture into it. Evenly scatter the grated cheese over the top. Bake for 35 to 40 minutes, or until the dish is cooked through the center and brown on the edges. Remove from the heat and let stand for 10 minutes. Cover the dish with a large, flat plate and turn it upside down. Fill the center with cilantro and parsley.

Serve hot.

Corn Bread

Corn bread has been around for about as long as the Deep South. It is a crumbly, gritty, semisweet mixture of baked cornmeal, eggs, butter, and sugar. Delicious when served hot with stews, or just buttered and eaten warm with sweet pickles or jam, it is a favorite in Cajun and Creole cuisine. There are a variety of ways to make it, with room for individual touches.

MAKES 1 LOAF

1 cup fine yellow cornmeal or fine polenta

1 cup flour

1 tablespoon baking powder

1/3 cup sugar

1 teaspoon salt

1 egg, beaten

1 cup milk

4 tablespoons butter, melted

Preheat the oven to 350°F/180°C.

Combine the cornmeal, flour, baking powder, sugar, and salt in a large mixing bowl. Make a well in the center, pour in the egg and milk, and whisk the liquid and dry ingredients together for 1 minute. Fold in the melted butter.

Grease a standard loaf pan and pour in the batter. Bake for 30 to 40 minutes. To test for doneness, insert a clean skewer in the corn bread; if it comes out clean, the bread is cooked. Remove from the oven and let stand for 10 minutes before turning out onto a wire rack.

Serve sliced and buttered.

New Orleans

New Orleans is a major seaport located on the Mississippi River, with access to the Gulf of Mexico. The city is famous for its French-influenced culture, as well as its street life and nightlife, the annual Mardi Gras celebration, and its Cajun, zydeco, jazz, and blues traditions dating from the nineteenth century.

Dirty Rice

This is Cajun food at its grassroots best. Hearty, inexpensive, and wholesome, it is found everywhere that Cajun cooking is served. This dish is actually a concoction of leftovers, and despite the name, the finished product is finger-licking good. Dirty rice looks mighty fine when served with flair on a bed of green leaf lettuce leaves, garnished with hard-boiled eggs, sliced tomatoes, chopped fresh chives, black olives, and carrot sticks.

SERVES 6 TO 8

1/4 pound (125 g) chicken livers, diced

1/4 pound (125 g) chicken hearts, diced

1/4 pound (125 g) chicken or turkey gizzards, skinned and diced

6 chicken wings, halved

1 tablespoon freshly grated nutmeg

1 tablespoon garlic powder combined with 1 teaspoon salt

1/4 cup flour

4 1/4 cups chicken stock

1 bay leaf

6 cloves garlic, crushed

Salt

1/2 teaspoon Tabasco sauce

1/2 teaspoon Worcestershire sauce

1 cup vegetable oil or bacon fat

3 red onions, diced

3 red chiles, diced (optional)

2 tomatoes, blanched, peeled, and diced

1 1/2 cups long-grain white or brown rice

2 teaspoons minced fresh oregano

1 teaspoon freshly ground black pepper

Pat all the meat dry with paper towels, and place in a large bowl. Mix together the nutmeg, garlic mixture, and flour. Season the meat with the mixture. Pour 1 cup of the chicken stock into a large pan. Add the bay leaf, half the garlic, a pinch of salt, and all the meat. Bring to a boil, decrease the heat, and simmer for 15 minutes, or until the meat is cooked through. Remove the bay leaf. Set aside to cool for 20 minutes. In a blender or food processor, blend the livers, hearts, and gizzards to make a rough paste. Add Tabasco and Worcestershire sauces and set aside.

In a very large pan, heat the oil and fry the seasoned chicken wings until they are nearly brown. Remove from the oil, drain, and set aside. In the same oil, fry the onions, chiles, and remaining garlic on low heat for about 5 minutes without browning the onions. Add the tomatoes and stir well. Cook for 3 to 4 minutes. Add the rice, oregano, black pepper, blended giblets, chicken wings, and remaining chicken stock. Stir well to mix, season to taste, decrease the heat, and cook for 30 to 40 minutes, or until all the liquid is absorbed and the rice and meats are soft and cooked.

Serve hot.

Drunken Crabs

Blue crabs are a favorite with many coastal and island cultures in the Caribbean region. This particular recipe has a Louisiana Creole touch. Louisiana Creoles are of Spanish and French origin, and their heritage is reflected in their cooking. They like stylishly presented food, frequently cooked with wine. Serve these crabs hot with crusty French bread and fresh salad.

SERVES 4

4 large blue crabs, uncooked

2 cups white wine or beer

2 cups fish stock (see Note), or 2 cups hot water mixed with 1 crushed fish bouillon cube

2 cloves garlic, crushed

1 tablespoon chopped fennel fronds

1 tablespoon chopped fresh dill

1 tablespoon chopped fresh chives

1 white onion, quartered

3 tomatoes, blanched and peeled

1 red bell pepper, seeded and quartered

4 teaspoons sugar

2 teaspoons unsalted butter

Salt

Freshly ground black pepper

2 to 4 teaspoons cornstarch blended with 6 tablespoons water

Preheat the oven to 350°F/180°C.

Bring plenty of water to boil in a large pan. Quickly drop in the crabs, cover, and simmer for 5 to 10 minutes, or until the shells are bright pink. Remove from the heat, drain, and rinse thoroughly in cold water. Put the crabs back in the empty pan, add the wine, fish stock, garlic, half the fennel, half the dill, half the chives, onion, tomatoes, bell pepper, sugar, and butter.

Bring to a boil and cook for 10 minutes, or until all the ingredients are softened. Remove from the heat.

Take out the crabs, arrange them in a large ovenproof dish, and bake for approximately 10 minutes.

Pour the sauce and vegetable mix into a blender and blend until smooth. Season with salt and pepper. Add the cornstarch mixture, return the sauce to the pan, and slowly stir on low heat until the sauce starts to thicken. Decrease the heat and cook for 1 to 2 minutes. Remove from the heat and pour the sauce over the crabs. Sprinkle with the remaining fennel, dill, and chives, and serve.

NOTE: To make your own fish stock, buy a variety of fish heads, tails, crab carcasses, claws, and so on from the fishmonger. Clean, put in a pan with 1 unpeeled onion, coarsely chopped; 4 cloves garlic, crushed; a handful of peppercorns; a lemon rind; 1 celery stalk, chopped; 8½ cups water; 1 bay leaf; 1 parsley sprig; and a pinch of salt. Boil slowly on low heat for 40 minutes to 1 hour. Let stand for 30 minutes, strain, and discard the solids.

Fish in Socks

Considering that Creole ancestry is grounded in fish-eating West Africa, it is not surprising that fish features prominently in Creole cooking. The exciting thing about Creole cuisine is how the traditional African recipes have evolved with the French, Spanish, Portuguese, and Native American influences. While the type of fish for this recipe depends on local and seasonal availability, it is best to choose a fleshy variety with few bones. This is a clever and tasty way to use the commonly leftover fish tails.

SERVES 4

16 fish tails, each about
   2 inches long with some
   flesh on them

1/2 cup corn oil

BATTER

1/2 cup flour

2 teaspoons dry mustard

1 teaspoon sweet paprika

1/2 teaspoon salt

1 tablespoon ketchup

1 teaspoon Worcestershire
   sauce

1 teaspoon mayonnaise

1/2 cup lager beer

1 teaspoon freshly squeezed
   lemon juice

1 egg

1 teaspoon minced gherkin

1 small white onion, finely
   diced

Rinse the fish tails and dry them on paper towels. In a mixing bowl, combine all the ingredients for the batter and stir well.

Heat the corn oil in a small pan until hot but not smoking. Dip each fish tail in batter, making sure you coat the whole piece. Gently shake off the excess batter, and fry in the hot oil for 5 minutes, or until crisp and brown all over.

Remove from the heat and drain on paper towels. Set aside and keep warm until all the fish tails are cooked.

Serve hot as an appetizer or snack with a small, crisp salad.

Mardi Gras

Mardi Gras—or versions such as Carnival or Val Val—is celebrated on most islands and regions to which African slaves were introduced.

Most preparations take place between the New Year and the beginning of Lent, culminating on Fat Tuesday, the day before Ash Wednesday. Originally, the festival was held by plantation owners and European colonizers who amalgamated their own festivities, such as the Shrove Tuesday end to the Lenten festival in France, with those rituals they had observed among their slave laborers.

The main attraction of the New Orleans's Mardi Gras is the enormous parade of floats, each sponsored by a Krewe, traditionally secret groups from which people of African, Jewish, and Asian ancestry were excluded. From among the Krewes, a Krewe king and queen are selected to ride on the royal float. In the past, these roles conferred great social status on the chosen pair. The king and queen and their entourage are richly dressed and, as part of the ritual, throw masses of junk jewelry mixed with valuable, specially minted coins to the crowds massed along the streets.

Following the Krewe parade are the alternative floats, created in parody by the black community. For the alternative floats, the king and queen wear Zulu dress, complete with leopard skins, and are attended by a Zulu entourage, including a witch doctor and a "Big Shot" character, who represents the wealth of Africa. Instead of gilt and coins, the Zulu king's entourage throws coconuts to the crowd.

It is fascinating to note that most African tribal festivals in West Africa, such as the Ghanaian Ga people's Homowo, the Ewe's Hogbotsotsu, and the Corn and Cassava Festival in Benin, culminate in parades of fetish priests and priestesses and are held on a Tuesday, just like Mardi Gras.

Honeyed Roast Leg of Pork

It is probable that the Cajuns or the Creoles' black slaves introduced pork into the diet of the Spanish Creoles of Louisiana. This recipe, usually served as a celebratory dish, probably came to Louisiana from the West Indies, where the African slaves would have learned to combine sweet and savory ingredients in a single dish—a practice that occurred only rarely in Africa itself. I recommend serving this with potato croquettes and vegetables roasted with the meat during the last 30 to 45 minutes of baking time.

SERVES 6 TO 8

1 leg of pork, 3 to 4 pounds
   (1.5 to 2 kg)

¼ cup vegetable oil

8 to 10 whole cloves

1 tablespoon cornstarch

2 teaspoons cayenne pepper

2 teaspoons ground cinnamon

1 teaspoon salt

1 tablespoon honey

3 cooking apples, peeled,
   cored, and quartered

Preheat the oven to 400°F/200°C.

Heavily score the skin of the leg of pork in a crisscross fashion. Place the oil and leg of pork in a baking dish, and stick the cloves firmly in between the scores in the skin, pushing them into the flesh underneath. Mix together the cornstarch, cayenne pepper, cinnamon, and salt. Rub the cornstarch mix all over the meat, making sure to season between the scores in the skin, too.

Bake, uncovered, for approximately 30 minutes. Turn the meat over, and bake the other side for another 30 minutes. Remove the meat from the baking dish. Drain the oil from the dish, and return the meat to the dish with the top of the leg up. Smear the honey all over the meat. Arrange the apples around the pork. Reduce the heat to 350°F/180°C, cover, and continue baking for 1 hour. Uncover the meat, turn up the heat to 375°F/190°C, and brown for 25 to 30 minutes, or until the meat is well cooked, tender, and brown.

Serve hot.

NOTE: As a guide, allow 25 to 30 minutes of baking time per 1 pound (500 g) of meat, plus an extra 25 to 30 minutes for browning. A leg of pork should take 1¼ to 1½ hours, plus browning time.

Glossary

Ablémamu: Ground roasted corn.

Akee: The edible fruit (when cooked) of seedpods of *Blighia sapida,* a tree common to Africa and the Caribbean. Available fresh or canned.

Apem: A baby plantain.

Aportoryiwa (Ghana): A round earthenware bowl of the Akan tribe.

Banku (Ghana): A cornmeal dumpling.

Bell Peppers: Also known as sweet peppers, these members of the *Capsicum* family, range in color from green to red, and yellow to orange.

Berbere (Ethiopia): A dry spice blend used for seasoning.

Cajun: A person born in Louisiana and descended from the French exiles of Acadia in Canada.

Callaloo: A green-leafed plant used like spinach in the West Indies.

Chinchin: Sweet West African pastry snacks.

Cilantro: Also referred to as coriander, cilantro is the bright green leaves and stems of the coriander plant.

Couscous: Durum wheat grains, commonly used in Moroccan cuisine.

Creole: Originally those of European (particularly French and Spanish) descent born in the West Indies, Spanish America, or the southern United States. Also a person born in the West Indies or Spanish America and descended from African slaves, as well as a person of mixed European and African ancestry in those places.

Dasheen: A term by which varieties of "spinach" are known in some Caribbean countries.

Dende Oil: A bright orange palm oil, high in saturated fat, which is popular in Brazilian cooking.

Eta (Ghana): Flat-ended Ashanti wooden masher.

Fufu: A variety of dumplings frequently made from root vegetables. Also known as *foofoo* in the West Indies.

Fuul Medames: A variety of brown broad bean, particularly popular in Egypt in a dish of the same name.

Gari: Coarse cassava powder. Also known as manioc, in Brazil as *farinhe de mandioca,* and in French-speaking countries as *farine de manioc.*

Green Onion: A member of the *Allium* family, these onions are also known as spring onions or scallions.

Gungo Peas: A Jamaican term for pigeon peas.

Hamine Eggs: These eggs, which are quite popular in Egypt, are boiled in their shells in stew or soups to take up the color and flavor.

Jollof: A West African pink risotto.

Kaawé: A traditional African cooking (meat-tenderizing) stone.

Kenkey: A general term for cornmeal dumpling, often wrapped in banana leaves (Fanti version) or corn leaves (Ga version).

Komi (Ghana): A corn dumpling (regional terminology for *kenkey).*

Kontomiré: The leaves of the cocoyam (taro root) plant.

Kubécake: West African coconut rum balls.

Loo (Ghana): Fish or meat (Ga regional terminology).

Makhrata: An Egyptian double-handed metal chopper.

Manioc: Coarse cassava powder. Also known as *gari* in West Africa, *farinhe de mandioca* in Brazil, and *farine de manioc* in French-speaking countries.

Mashamba: A variety of Zimbabwean pumpkin.

Mchicha: A leafy plant similar to spinach; a staple food in Tanzania.

Mealie-meal: A southern African staple, mealie-meal is thickened corn porridge.

Millet: Small, edible grains from a wheatlike grass that is widely cultivated for food and forage crop. Millet is extremely popular throughout Africa.

Mitmita (Ethiopia): A variety of yellow pepper.

Moi-Moi: A Nigerian savory bean pâté.

Palm Oil: Extremely high in saturated fat, this distinctive tasting oil is gained by extraction from the pulp of the fruit of the African palm. If you can't find palm oil, substitute 1 cup vegetable oil and add to it 4 teaspoons ground turmeric.

Plantains: Related to the banana and commonly known as the "cooking banana," plantains are usually cooked when green and have a mild flavor.

Rapoko: Red millet flour.

Sadza (Zimbabwe): A white corn or millet dumpling.

Samna: Rich, clarified Egyptian cooking butter.

Shitor (Ghana): Chile sambal.

Shrimp: This popular shellfish comes in various sizes, ranging from miniature to jumbo. Shrimp is found in the cuisines of countries all over the world and is often sold under the name "prawns."

Swiss Chard: This green is often used like spinach, and is alternately known as silver beet.

Yellow Onion: A mild- to strong-flavored onion, excellent in a variety of dishes. Also known as brown onion.

Wot: An Ethiopian stew.

Recommended Reading

Barrett, Leonard. *The Sun and the Drum*. Kingston: Sangster's Book Stores in association with Heinemann Educational Books, 1976.

Bennett, Olivia. *Village in Egypt*. London: A & C Black, 1983.

Bourne, M. J., G.W. Lennox, and S.A. Seddou. *Fruits and Vegetables of the Caribbean*. Caribbean Pocket Natural History Series. London: The Macmillan Press Ltd., 1988.

Crowder, Michael. *West Africa Under Colonial Rule*. London: Hutchinson and Co., Ltd., 1968.

Dede, Alice. *Ghanaian Favorite Dishes*. McCarthy, Accara, Ghana: Anowno Educational Publications, 1999.

Fuller, B.G. *Ghanian Cookery*. London: New Millennium, 1998.

Hafner, Dorinda. *Dorinda's Taste of the Caribbean*. Berkeley, California: Ten Speed Press, 1996.

_____. *United Tastes of America*. London: Ebury Press, 1997.

_____. *Tastes of Britain*. London: Kyle Cathie Limited, 1998.

Parry, J.H., Philip Sherlock, and Anthony Maingot. *A Short History of the West Indies.* London: The Macmillan Press Ltd., 1994.

Thimodent, Robert. *Tradition Culinaire Creole/Creole Cooking Style.* Guadeloupe: D.F. Editions, 1995.

Waters, Erika J., ed. *New Writing from the Caribbean.* London: The Macmillan Press Ltd., 1994.

Index

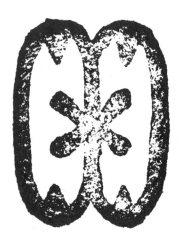 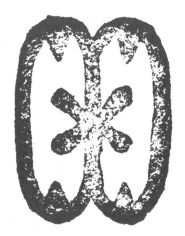 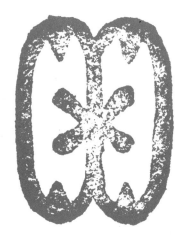